Harm Reduction:
Public Health Strategies

Other Books of Related Interest

Opposing Viewpoints Series

Addiction
Chemical Dependency
Medical Marijuana
Prescription Drug Abuse

At Issue Series

Alcohol Abuse
Are Americans Overmedicated?
Do Abstinence Programs Work?
Prescription Drugs

Current Controversies Series

Drug Legalization
Medical Ethics
Medical Marijuana
Prescription Drugs

"Congress shall make
no law … abridging
the freedom of speech,
or of the press."

First Amendment to the US Constitution

The basic foundation of our democracy is the First Amendment guarantee of freedom of expression. The Opposing Viewpoints series is dedicated to the concept of this basic freedom and the idea that it is more important to practice it than to enshrine it.

OPPOSING
VIEWPOINTS®
SERIES

Harm Reduction: Public Health Strategies

Barbara Krasner, Book Editor

GREENHAVEN
PUBLISHING

Published in 2019 by Greenhaven Publishing, LLC
353 3rd Avenue, Suite 255, New York, NY 10010

First Edition

Articles in Greenhaven Publishing anthologies are often edited for length to meet page
requirements. In addition, original titles of these works are changed to clearly present
the main thesis and to explicitly indicate the author's opinion. Every effort is made to
ensure that Greenhaven Publishing accurately reflects the original intent of the authors.
Every effort has been made to trace the owners of the copyrighted material.

Cover image: Richard Lautens/Toronto Star via Getty Images

Library of Congress Cataloging-in-Publication Data

Names: Krasner, Barbara, editor.
Title: Harm reduction : public health strategies / Barbara Krasner, book editor.
Description: First edition. | New York : Greenhaven Publishing, 2019. |
  Series: Opposing viewpoints | Includes bibliographical references and
  index. | Audience: Grades 9–12.
Identifiers: LCCN 2018025856| ISBN 9781534504134 (library bound) | ISBN
  9781534504370 (pbk.)
Subjects: LCSH: Substance abuse—Treatment—United States—Juvenile
  literature. | Substance abuse—United States—Juvenile literature. |
  Addicts—Services for—United States—Juvenile literature. | Public
  health—United States—Juvenile literature.
Classification: LCC RC564.65 .H367 2019 | DDC 362.290973—dc23
LC record available at https://lccn.loc.gov/2018025856

Manufactured in the United States of America

Website: http://greenhavenpublishing.com

Contents

The Importance of Opposing Viewpoints

Perhaps every generation experiences a period in time in which the populace seems especially polarized, starkly divided on the important issues of the day and gravitating toward the far ends of the political spectrum and away from a consensus-facilitating middle ground. The world that today's students are growing up in and that they will soon enter into as active and engaged citizens is deeply fragmented in just this way. Issues relating to terrorism, immigration, women's rights, minority rights, race relations, health care, taxation, wealth and poverty, the environment, policing, military intervention, the proper role of government—in some ways, perennial issues that are freshly and uniquely urgent and vital with each new generation—are currently roiling the world.

If we are to foster a knowledgeable, responsible, active, and engaged citizenry among today's youth, we must provide them with the intellectual, interpretive, and critical-thinking tools and experience necessary to make sense of the world around them and of the all-important debates and arguments that inform it. After all, the outcome of these debates will in large measure determine the future course, prospects, and outcomes of the world and its peoples, particularly its youth. If they are to become successful members of society and productive and informed citizens, students need to learn how to evaluate the strengths and weaknesses of someone else's arguments, how to sift fact from opinion and fallacy, and how to test the relative merits and validity of their own opinions against the known facts and the best possible available information. The landmark series Opposing Viewpoints has been providing students with just such critical-thinking skills and exposure to the debates surrounding society's most urgent contemporary issues for many years, and it continues to serve this essential role with undiminished commitment, care, and rigor.

The key to the series's success in achieving its goal of sharpening students' critical-thinking and analytic skills resides in its title—

Opposing Viewpoints. In every intriguing, compelling, and engaging volume of this series, readers are presented with the widest possible spectrum of distinct viewpoints, expert opinions, and informed argumentation and commentary, supplied by some of today's leading academics, thinkers, analysts, politicians, policy makers, economists, activists, change agents, and advocates. Every opinion and argument anthologized here is presented objectively and accorded respect. There is no editorializing in any introductory text or in the arrangement and order of the pieces. No piece is included as a "straw man," an easy ideological target for cheap point-scoring. As wide and inclusive a range of viewpoints as possible is offered, with no privileging of one particular political ideology or cultural perspective over another. It is left to each individual reader to evaluate the relative merits of each argument—as he or she sees it, and with the use of ever-growing critical-thinking skills—and grapple with his or her own assumptions, beliefs, and perspectives to determine how convincing or successful any given argument is and how the reader's own stance on the issue may be modified or altered in response to it.

This process is facilitated and supported by volume, chapter, and selection introductions that provide readers with the essential context they need to begin engaging with the spotlighted issues, with the debates surrounding them, and with their own perhaps shifting or nascent opinions on them. In addition, guided reading and discussion questions encourage readers to determine the authors' point of view and purpose, interrogate and analyze the various arguments and their rhetoric and structure, evaluate the arguments' strengths and weaknesses, test their claims against available facts and evidence, judge the validity of the reasoning, and bring into clearer, sharper focus the reader's own beliefs and conclusions and how they may differ from or align with those in the collection or those of their classmates.

Research has shown that reading comprehension skills improve dramatically when students are provided with compelling, intriguing, and relevant "discussable" texts. The subject matter of these collections could not be more compelling, intriguing, or urgently relevant to today's students and the world they are poised to inherit. The anthologized articles and the reading and discussion questions that are included with them also provide the basis for stimulating, lively, and passionate classroom debates. Students who are compelled to anticipate objections to their own arguments and identify the flaws in those of an opponent read more carefully, think more critically, and steep themselves in relevant context, facts, and information more thoroughly. In short, using discussable text of the kind provided by every single volume in the Opposing Viewpoints series encourages close reading, facilitates reading comprehension, fosters research, strengthens critical thinking, and greatly enlivens and energizes classroom discussion and participation. The entire learning process is deepened, extended, and strengthened.

For all of these reasons, Opposing Viewpoints continues to be exactly the right resource at exactly the right time—when we most need to provide readers with the critical-thinking tools and skills that will not only serve them well in school but also in their careers and their daily lives as decision-making family members, community members, and citizens. This series encourages respectful engagement with and analysis of opposing viewpoints and fosters a resulting increase in the strength and rigor of one's own opinions and stances. As such, it helps make readers "future ready," and that readiness will pay rich dividends for the readers themselves, for the citizenry, for our society, and for the world at large.

Introduction

"*Whether it is the rapid rise of prescription opioid addiction or the longstanding challenge of alcohol dependence, substance misuse and substance use disorders can—and do— prevent people from living healthy and productive lives.*"

—*US Surgeon General, Vivek H. Murthy[1]*

The numbers are staggering. The US federal government estimated in 2016 that nearly 22.5 million people reported using an illegal drug the previous year. More than 20 million people suffer from substance use disorders. Seventy-eight people die from opioid overdose every single day.[2] Yet, there is a potential solution to this enormous problem—harm reduction.

But experts have not agreed about harm reduction strategies for substance abuse since its inception, whether they believe harm reduction began in the 1920s or in the 1980s. Irrespective of its origins, harm reduction's goal is to help drug and alcohol users lead healthier lives by reducing or eliminating their dependence on substance use. Achieving this goal requires the participation and commitment of users, their loved ones, medical professionals, law enforcement, local and state government, and federal agencies.

Since its inception, harm reduction has stirred controversy, and many of its practices have received both criticism and debate. For example, there are pros and cons about harm reduction's strategies. While a number of solutions, such as e-cigarettes, Hepatitis C drugs, methadone maintenance therapy, syringe access, and buprenorphine to reduce opioid use, result in a less harmful form of use, these solutions can also cause dangerous side effects. In addition, in taking responsibility for their own health using harm reduction strategies, substance abusers might also be setting themselves up for failure. On the other hand, medical professionals, either in private practice or at hospitals, may inhibit user success. They may hold negative biases against their patients. Emergency room visits may prove to be less effective than harm reduction. These issues present both sides of whether harm reduction strategies can be successful.

At the core, the question arises whether users of illegal substances have a right to quality health care. The Affordable Health Care Act and access to a universal health care system are ways in which substance abusers can get the help they need. Yet, the current Trump administration believes quality health care is a privilege, not a right. People with lower incomes may end up paying more money for less coverage, causing substance abusers to bypass professional help. To alleviate this, users and medical professionals must work together to make harm reduction successful. But such an action requires communication and an ability to rise above shame, racial prejudice, and other social stigmas. For example, the Institute of Family Health in New York uses a two-page Harm Reduction and Safety Recovery Plan for underinsured patients in its twenty-six centers. The plan takes into account whether the goal is harm reduction or abstinence.

Researchers continue to study whether harm reduction or abstinence is the more successful approach to help steer users away from abusive behaviors. While harm reduction is explicitly intended to reduce harmful drug use, advocates for abstinence maintain that permitting continued use is an enabling behavior that stands in the way of positive change. Harm reduction advocates, on the other hand, claim that complete abstinence leads to relapse of substance abuse, and therefore, failure. These advocates also argue that each user as a client deserves a customized treatment plan, taking into consideration each user's current state.

Aside from medical help, law enforcement can either help or hinder a user's success in reducing reliance on substances. Yet, medical professionals may view such involvement as harmful, because it may subject clients to detention, incarceration, and physical torture. On the other hand, organizations such as Law Enforcement and HIV Network (LEAHN) work to bring these two factions together for the users' benefit. This network, for example, provides educational programs and knowledge-sharing resources to foster public health partnerships locally and globally.

Through diverse perspectives, the contributors in *Opposing Viewpoints: Harm Reduction: Public Health Strategies* examine negative stereotypes of drug users and other issues in chapters titled "Are Harm Reduction Strategies Successful?," "Do Drug Users Have a Right to Quality Health Care?," "Is Abstinence the Only Successful Method of Recovery?," and "Does Law Enforcement Help or Hinder Harm Reduction?" The questions surrounding the medical, social, and legal perspectives of allowing drug users to continue to use at minimized levels remain subjects of intense scrutiny and vigorous debate among health care professionals, scholars, journalists, and researchers.

Notes

1. U.S. Department of Health and Human Services Office of the Surgeon General, "Facing Addiction in America: The Surgeon General's Report on Alcohol, Drugs, and Health" (Washington, DC: HHS, 2016), V.

2. Ibid., III.

CHAPTER 1

Are Harm Reduction Strategies Successful?

Chapter Preface

H arm reduction is the safe and managed use of drugs to encourage a more healthful form of use and to reduce opioid use. Such solutions include Suboxone (or buprenorphine), methadone maintenance therapy, syringe exchange, and e-cigarettes. When combined with other therapies, such as behavioral intervention, harm reduction can prove successful. However, several factors can threaten the success of harm reduction programs. Among medical professionals, for example, unconscious racial biases result in the stereotyping of patients and compromise their care.

At its core, harm reduction is based on the philosophy that patients are in charge of their own bodies and they must live with the consequences of their choices, good or bad. Many are not ready for an institutionalized approach of detoxification through abstinence because of previously poor experiences in a hospital setting and/or the nature of their withdrawal symptoms, which can seem horrific. Given this, they may also not be prepared to take responsibility for their own conditions and may actually harm themselves further.

On the other hand, emergency room visits—because opioid users may tend to avoid medical treatment until infections or other problems become physically unbearable—may make matters worse. Interviews among patients given Suboxone demonstrate the drug's side effects that can affect the patient's mental state. When not properly or consistently supervised by medical staff, that mental state could have disastrous results not only for patients, but also for the people around them.

The following chapter examines whether harm reduction strategies are indeed successful and identifies potential problem areas and their consequences. The authors of the viewpoints present varying opinions on the practice of harm reduction strategies in hospital settings and call for a range of solutions.

> *"As with other chronic, relapsing medical conditions, treatment can manage the symptoms of substance use disorders and prevent relapse."*

Successful Recovery Requires a Blend of Treatment Options

U.S. Department of Health & Human Services

In the following excerpted viewpoint, the US Department of Health & Human Services argues that effective treatments for drug and alcohol addiction are available. It contends that both medicinal and behavioral treatments are necessary for recovery. It further posits that the Affordable Health Care Act makes treatment accessible and that the criminal justice system is positioned and ready to focus on treatment rather than imprisonment of users. The US Department of Health & Human Services seeks to protect the health and well-being of Americans, delivering and fostering advances in public health services.

As you read, consider the following questions:

1. Are behavioral interventions necessary among abusers of drugs and alcohol?
2. How many Americans are living with their addiction in remission?
3. Are medications alone effective in treating alcohol and drug addiction?

"Facing Addiction in America," U.S. Department of Health & Human Services.

The problem of alcohol and drug misuse in the United States is serious and pervasive. However, despite the challenges described above, this is also a time of great hope and opportunity:

- Research on alcohol and drug use, and addiction, has led to an increase of knowledge and to one clear conclusion: Addiction to alcohol or drugs is a chronic but treatable brain disease that requires medical intervention, not moral judgment.
- Policies and programs have been developed that are effective in preventing alcohol and drug misuse and reducing its negative effects.
- Effective treatments for substance use disorders are available. Evidence-based treatments—both medications and behavioral therapies—can save lives and restore people's health, well-being, and functioning, as well as reduce the spread of infectious disease and lessen other consequences.
- Support services such as mutual aid groups (e.g., Alcoholics Anonymous), recovery housing, and recovery coaches are increasingly available to help people in the long and often difficult task of maintaining recovery after treatment.
- Health care reform efforts are creating new opportunities to increase access to prevention and treatment services to improve public health. Health insurers that participate in the new Health Care Marketplace must now cover costs related to mental health and substance use disorder services, including behavioral health treatment, and may not apply limitations on those benefits that are more restrictive than limitations applied on the benefits for medical and surgical services. Other incentives are encouraging general health systems to control costs, improve outcomes, and reduce readmissions by addressing patients' substance use. Transformations in the health care landscape are supporting integration of substance use disorder treatment with general health care in ways that will better address the needs of the millions of people suffering from these disorders.

- The criminal justice system is engaged in efforts to place non-violent drug offenders in treatment instead of jail, to improve the delivery of evidence-based treatment for incarcerated persons, and to coordinate care in the community when inmates are released.

Together, these changes are leading to a new landscape of care for alcohol and drug misuse problems in America, and to new hope for millions of people who suffer from them.

[...]

Treatment for substance use disorders can take many different forms and may be delivered in a range of settings varying in intensity. In all cases, though, the goals of treatment for substance use disorders are similar to treatment for any medical condition: to reduce the major symptoms of the illness and return the patient to a state of full functioning. Ideally, services are not "one size fits all" but are tailored to the unique needs of the individual. Treatment must be provided for an adequate length of time and should address the patient's substance use as well as related health and social consequences that could contribute to the risk of relapse, including connecting the patient to social support, housing, employment, and other wrap-around services.

Screening for substance misuse in health care settings including primary, psychiatric, urgent, and emergency care is the first step in identifying behaviors that put individuals at risk for harms, including for developing a substance use disorder, and to identify patients with existing substance use disorders. Screening and brief intervention for alcohol in adults has been shown to be effective;31 and screening for substance use and mental health problems is recommended by major health organizations for both adults and adolescents. Brief advice or therapy would follow a positive screen and be tailored to an individual's specific needs; referral can be made to specialty treatment depending on severity.

Treatment for all substance use disorders—including alcohol, marijuana, cocaine, heroin or other opioid use disorders, among others—should include one or more types of behavioral interventions delivered in individual, group, and sometimes family settings. Evidence-based behavioral interventions may seek to increase patients' motivation to change, increase their self-efficacy (their belief in their ability to carry out actions that can achieve their goals), or help them identify and change disrupted behavior patterns and abnormal thinking.

The intensity of substance use disorder treatment services falls along a continuum. For people with mild substance use disorders, counseling services provided through primary care or other outpatient settings with an intensity of one or two counseling sessions per week may be sufficient while residential treatment may be necessary for people with a severe substance use disorder. Residential treatment was designed to provide a highly controlled environment with a high density of daily services. Ideally, people who receive treatment in residential settings participate in step-down services following the residential stay. Step-down services may include intensive outpatient or other outpatient counseling and recovery support services (RSS) to promote and encourage patients to independently manage their condition.

Medications are also available to help treat people addicted to alcohol or opioids. Research is underway to develop new medications to treat other substance use disorders, such as addiction to marijuana or cocaine, but none have yet been approved by the U.S. Food and Drug Administration (FDA). The available medications do not by themselves restore the addicted brain to health, but they can support an individual's treatment process and recovery by preventing the substance from having pleasurable effects in the brain, by causing an unpleasant reaction when the substance is used, or by controlling symptoms of withdrawal and craving. Widening access to highly effective medications for treating opioid addiction—methadone, buprenorphine, and naltrexone— has been identified by United States public health authorities as an essential part of tackling America's current prescription opioid and heroin crisis.

In summary: Treatment is effective. As with other chronic, relapsing medical conditions, treatment can manage the symptoms of substance use disorders and prevent relapse. Rates of relapse following treatment for substance use disorders are comparable to those of other chronic illnesses such as diabetes, asthma, and hypertension. More than 25 million individuals with a previous substance use disorder are in remission and living healthy, productive lives.

However, many people seek or are referred to substance use treatment only after a crisis, such as an overdose, or through involvement with the criminal justice system. With any other health condition like heart disease, detecting problems and offering treatment only after a crisis is not considered good medicine. Integrating screening into general medical settings will make it easier to identify those in need of treatment and engage them in the appropriate level of care before a crisis occurs. Overall, the need is for a stepped care model, in which mild to moderate substance use disorders are detected and addressed in general health care settings and severe disorders are treated by specialists using a chronic care model coordinated with primary care. The good news is that the existing health care system is well poised to help address the health consequences of alcohol and drug misuse and substance use disorders.

[...]

By adopting an evidence-based public health approach, America has the opportunity to take genuinely effective steps to prevent and treat substance-related issues. Such an approach can prevent substance initiation or escalation from use to a disorder, and thus reduce the number of people suffering with addiction; it can shorten the duration of illness for sufferers; and it can reduce the number of substance-related deaths. A public health approach will also reduce collateral damage created by substance misuse, such as infectious disease transmission and motor vehicle crashes. Thus, promoting much wider adoption of appropriate evidence-based prevention, treatment, and recovery strategies needs to be a top public health priority.

Making this change will require a major cultural shift in the way we think about, talk about, look at, and act toward people with substance use disorders. Negative attitudes and ways of talking about substance misuse and substance use disorders can be entrenched, but it is possible to change social attitudes. This has been done many times in the past: Cancer and HIV used to be surrounded by fear and judgment, now they are regarded by many as simply medical conditions. This has helped people become comfortable talking about their concerns with their doctors, widening access to prevention and treatment. By coming together as a society with the resolve to do so, it is similarly possible to change attitudes toward substance misuse and substance use disorders. There is a strong scientific as well as moral case for addressing substance use disorders with a public health model that focuses on reducing both health and social justice disparities, and it aligns strongly with an economic case. Now is the time to make this change, for the health and well-being of all Americans.

> *"It's not that abstinence is not a goal, but the aim of MAT is rather to stop the devastating consequences of this terrible illness and keep the patient alive and engaged in the process of treatment."*

Treating Addiction with Medication Should Be Carefully Considered

Scott Teitelbaum

In the following viewpoint, Scott Teitelbaum argues that medically-assisted treatment for opioid addiction, while not a singular solution, should be considered as a part of a larger treatment plan. The author points out that doctors prescribe medication for other medical conditions, yet there is a stigma to doing the same for substance abuse, for which abstinence is often considered the only course. Teitelbaum is a professor of psychiatry at the University of Florida's College of Medicine, where he serves as vice chair of the psychiatry department, chief of addiction medicine, and medical director of the UF Health Florida Recovery Center.

"Why Treating Addiction with Medication Should Be Carefully Considered," by Scott Teitelbaum, The Conversation, February 6, 2018. https://theconversation.com/why-treating-addiction-with-medication-should-be-carefully-considered-89010 Licensed under CC BY-ND 4.0 International.

As you read, consider the following questions:

1. What is MAT?
2. What percent of the world's prescribed pain medications does the US use?
3. What is buprenorphine, according to the viewpoint?

When a patient has diabetes, doctors typically prescribe insulin, along with diet and exercise. When a patient has high blood pressure, we prescribe medication, and we also reinforce the importance of healthy eating, exercise, weight loss and quitting smoking.

When it comes to the disease of opioid addiction, however, some critics describe the use of medication as merely substituting one opioid for another, preferring instead total abstinence. Others see pharmacotherapy as the most critical component in treating the current opioid epidemic.

More than 2 million people in the U.S. have an opioid abuse disorder, yet only a small fraction actually receive treatment. For those who do, our society uses a specific term to refer to the medication part: "medication-assisted treatment," or MAT.

The medications currently approved to treat opioid addiction act on the brain's opioid receptors by either substituting as a less rewarding drug or blocking the euphoric effects of opioids. In either case, the goal is to decrease the use of the more addictive and lethal opioids and stop the cycle of addiction.

As with any illness, the goal should be to have patients on the least amount of medication needed. But sometimes, as with diabetes or heart disease, medications are needed in concert with other treatment.

To me, even the name "medication-assisted treatment" is problematic: We're treating addiction differently than other diseases, due to the stigma that's always surrounded it.

As medical director of the UF Health Florida Recovery Center, I consider medication to often be part of a multi-pronged treatment approach for many patients suffering from opioid addiction. Each person is different, and we need to individualize treatment. While using medicine is often important, it is not a panacea. Here's why we need to carefully consider how and when we use medications, for all types of addiction and mental health issues.

A Nation with a Long History of Opioid Use

Prior to the Civil War, morphine was synthesized to treat pain. This, combined with advancements in anesthesia, exposed a great number of soldiers to opioids. Following the war, addiction was called "the soldier's disease" or "the Army's disease."

Soldiers said the drug not only relieved physical pain, but also the emotional pain of their wartime experience. Even then, the wounded and those who treated them recognized that opioids relieved both physical and psychic pain.

Our country's first heroin epidemic began in the late 1800s. This was followed by the Harrison Narcotics Act of 1914, which stated it was not in good faith for physicians to treat heroin addiction with morphine, as addiction was not considered a disease then. It was illegal for physicians to use opioids to treat opioid addiction, and many physicians went to prison when they did.

In the 1920s and '30s, people who were caught "doctor shopping" to get opioid prescriptions were sent to "narcotic farms" in Lexington, Kentucky, and Fort Worth, Texas, for treatment. Once released, most relapsed.

In the 1950s and '60s, U.S. doctors began the practice of methadone maintenance, initiated in large part to reduce urban crime.

Another shift in opioid usage happened in 2001. The Joint Commission on Accreditation of Healthcare Organizations first established standards for pain assessment and treatment. Though the standards did not state that pain needed to be treated like a vital sign, some organizations implemented programs by making pain "the fifth vital sign." Doctors began to treat pain more liberally, exposing more sufferers of pain to opioids.

Today, the U.S. has about 5 percent of the world's population, and we use an estimated 90 percent of the world's prescribed pain medications.

Today's opioid crisis has been the deadliest yet. More than 64,000 Americans lost their lives to drug overdose in 2016 – about two-thirds were from opioids. Most of the other overdose deaths were from central nervous system depressants like Xanax and alcohol, highlighting the importance of not forgetting the risk of other drugs.

Pain Medications as Gateways

For those who become addicted to painkillers, heroin becomes attractive because it is cheaper and widely available. Because of this, overdose deaths from prescription opioids decreased about 2010, while there was a precipitous rise in overdoses of heroin and fentanyl, a synthetic narcotic sometimes sold on the street as heroin.

Fentanyl is extremely potent; it's used in the operating room to put people under anesthesia. The sharpest increase in number of deaths – an estimated 20,000 deaths – was due to fentanyl.

Undoing the Damage a Slow Process

Modern-day MAT stems from the 2002 Food and Drug Administration approval of buprenorphine for the treatment of opioid withdrawal and maintenance. Buprenorphine is a partial opiate agonist, or a drug that operates as an opioid, but with a ceiling effect to help significantly decrease the chance of respiratory arrest from overdose. Unlike methadone, which must be dispensed in a highly structured clinic, buprenorphine can be prescribed in a doctor's office on an outpatient basis.

According to the National Institute on Drug Abuse, medications are an important element for many patients with opioid addiction. They are especially effective when combined with counseling, other behavioral therapies and 12-step recovery programs like Narcotics Anonymous.

Principles of Harm Reduction

Harm reduction is a set of practical strategies and ideas aimed at reducing negative consequences associated with drug use. Harm Reduction is also a movement for social justice built on a belief in, and respect for, the rights of people who use drugs.

Harm reduction incorporates a spectrum of strategies from safer use, to managed use to abstinence to meet drug users "where they're at," addressing conditions of use along with the use itself. Because harm reduction demands that interventions and policies designed to serve drug users reflect specific individual and community needs, there is no universal definition of or formula for implementing harm reduction.

However, HRC considers the following principles central to harm reduction practice.

- Accepts, for better and or worse, that licit and illicit drug use is part of our world and chooses to work to minimize its harmful effects rather than simply ignore or condemn them.
- Understands drug use as a complex, multi-faceted phenomenon that encompasses a continuum of behaviors from severe abuse to total abstinence, and acknowledges that some ways of using drugs are clearly safer than others.
- Establishes quality of individual and community life and well-being–not necessarily cessation of all drug use–as the criteria for successful interventions and policies.

"Principles of Harm Reduction," **Harm Reduction Coalition.**

Research shows that MAT results in what we addiction specialists call harm reduction. This means that while some of these patients may not be ready to be opioid-free, we want to keep them alive and achieving the greatest level of functioning. We don't want them engaging in self-destructive behaviors like relapsing to street drugs, committing crimes, overdosing or acquiring infectious diseases like HIV. And there's good evidence, some of which was presented as recently as Jan. 23, 2018, that medications have helped decrease HIV, hepatitis C and crime, as well as improve function.

It's not that abstinence is not a goal, but the aim of MAT is rather to stop the devastating consequences of this terrible illness and keep the patient alive and engaged in the process of treatment. Many have serious, co-occurring health problems, such as mental illness and a history of trauma. They may not yet have the ability to deal with the physical and emotional discomfort of being opioid-free.

In the last two years, the FDA has approved new formulations of buprenorphine to treat opioid addiction. One is a once-monthly injection and another an implant that can be effective up to six months. These longer-acting options can stabilize a patient by decreasing cravings, which then discourages use.

Larger Treatment Plans Are Important

It is true, nonetheless, that if not done carefully, these MAT medications can be abused themselves. If taken with other drugs or in larger amounts, these drugs can cause overdoses, too.

In my view, the goal should be prescribing the least amount of medication one needs. Regardless of what medication is used during treatment, we should be pushing patients to be the best versions of themselves and to live their fullest lives possible. I favor scrapping the debate over whether we are abstinence-based or medication-based and instead asking, "What does this individual need?"

Then one day, I hope, we can shake the "medication-assisted" and just call it what it is: treatment.

"Harm reduction is not about being
'soft on drugs,' nor about reducing
the consequences of drug use. It's
about allowing people the liberty to
make their own choices about what
they put in their bodies and to take
responsibility for those choices."

The Marriage of Harm Reduction and Conservatism Promotes Personal Choice

Tessie Castillo

In the following viewpoint, Tessie Castillo argues that the federal government has wasted taxpayer dollars in the war against drugs, because drugs are more plentiful than ever. She maintains that people are in charge of their own bodies and must take responsibility for their choices. She also contends that harm reduction advocates take this to heart, and by doing so, they have found common ground with conservatives. Castillo serves as the Advocacy and Communications Coordinator for the North Carolina Harm Reduction Coalition. She is a registered lobbyist and has fought for new drug policy laws, including the legalization of syringe exchange programs.

"A Conservative Argument for Harm Reduction," by Tessie Castillo, Advocacy and Communications Coordinator for the North Carolina Harm Reduction Coalition, Tessie Castillo, January 13, 2014. Reprinted by permission.

As you read, consider the following questions:

1. According to this viewpoint, who is ultimately responsible for drug abuse?
2. Was President Reagan's war on drugs successful?
3. According to this viewpoint, what is the harm reduction philosophy?

L ast year the North Carolina Harm Reduction Coalition surprised the nation by working with conservative legislators to pass two new drug policy laws in their state. But although the harm reduction philosophy of "meeting people where they are at" is sometimes at odds with conservatives' stricter approach to drug use, the alliance shouldn't have come as a surprise. In fact, the two ideologies frequently align by emphasizing personal responsibility, fiscal prudence, and the value of human life at all stages.

Like conservatism, the harm reduction philosophy stresses that people should have the right to do what they wish with their own bodies and to assume the responsibility for those decisions. Take alcohol, for example. Under our current laws, people can choose to be responsible or irresponsible with alcohol. Many choose not to drink at all. Others drink only in social situations or on weekends. And for some, alcoholism may be a lifelong battle against a disease that threatens to take everything from them. But it is their battle to fight, win or lose. Harm reductionists and conservatives would both agree it is not the government's job to interfere unless the person poses a threat to others, such as through drunk driving or violence while under the influence. Even then, it is the act of recklessness or violence for which the person might be punished, not for the act of drinking. Arresting everyone who drank, regardless of how much, how often, or whether they posed a risk to others, would mean costly arrests, imprisonment, court arraignments, lawyers, appeals, and other expenses that ultimately fall on the taxpayer. More importantly it would mean unnecessary government involvement in a personal matter. And yet this is exactly what we've done with drugs. In the United States we arrest everyone for the use of certain drugs, regardless of how much they use, how often, or whether that use puts others at risk. Since the 1980s when President Reagan adopted a zero tolerance policy on drug use, we have built more prisons, upped our law enforcement quotas, and poured money into the bottomless pit that is the court system. We've spent more than $60 billion since the so-called War on Drugs began under President Nixon, yet drugs are cheaper and more plentiful than ever before. A conservative might call this wasteful government spending. So would a harm reductionist.

"Any policy that inhibits freedom of choice, and costs the government more tax dollars is deeply flawed and unacceptable to a good conservative," says Aleq Boyle, National Director for Civic Society America. "We have endured several generations of a deeply flawed expensive and failed policies related to "Drug Wars" and have only created false economies of private prisons, poorly focused law enforcement directives, and we have increased the social and health burdens upon families and victims in the name of 'justice.'"

Fear has played a large role in the continuation of our costly, ineffective drug policies; it's a lucrative business for anyone looking to sell news stories or win votes. Fear of drugs and people who use them have caused us to allow government interference in our personal lives and also to neglect another great conservative tenet, the sanctity of human life. Arguably, to be pro-life is to believe in the innate value and potential of all people, yet society is often quick to dismiss drug users as "worthless" or "undeserving" unless they get clean. We don't do this for any other behaviors. We don't say people with anger issues are worthless unless they stop being angry. We don't say people who are overweight deserve misery unless they get thin. While drugs can cause great harm, who among us doesn't have a habit or personality trait that is at times harmful to ourselves and those around us? It's up to each of us to work on self-improvement, but we are still valuable people during the process, even if we fail.

Thanks in part to greater public awareness about the drug war, Americans are beginning to wake up to the inconsistencies in our national drug policy. Some states have changed their laws to emphasize treatment over incarceration or life over death by overdose. And in many, such as North Carolina, harm reductionists and conservatives have worked together to make these changes. Harm reduction is not about being "soft on drugs," nor about reducing the consequences of drug use. It's about allowing people the liberty to make their own choices about what they put in their bodies and to take responsibility for those choices. It's about exercising restraint when it comes to excessive government spending on prisons and courts. It's about believing in the value and potential of every human being no matter where they are on the drug use continuum. Some might say the harm reductionists and conservatives have finally found common ground. But I think the similarities were there all along.

| "*Expecting people to detox to access services is seen as a bygone approach.*"

Inconsistent Hospital Policies and Tactics Threatens Recovery

Wendy Glauser, Jeremy Petch, and Mike Tierney

In the following viewpoint, excerpted for length, Wendy Glauser, Jeremy Petch, and Mike Tierney argue that medical professionals need to be consistent in their treatment of opioid users to facilitate recovery. Through interviews with medical staff and patients, they maintain that forced detox ultimately results in setbacks and even overdosing. Glauser is an award-winning journalist focusing on health and science. Petch is manager of special projects at the Li Ka Shing Knowledge Institute of St. Michael's Hospital in Toronto. Tierney is Vice President of Clinical Programs at The Ottawa Hospital.

As you read, consider the following questions:

1. How do prior negative experiences in a hospital setting affect opioid users?
2. Can detox in a hospital stop addiction?
3. Do stigmas against drug abusers impact the level of help they get in a hospital?

"Hospital Policies Put the Lives of People Who Inject Drugs at Risk, Say Experts," by Wendy Glauser, Jeremy Petch and Mike Tierney, Healthy Debate, July 21, 2016. Reprinted by permission.

In 2015, Shawn was in the hospital with an abscess on his spine and a life-threatening blood infection. After waiting more than a day in the emergency department, he was withdrawing from heroin—sweating profusely, extremely anxious and in excruciating pain. "It felt like someone was crushing my skull. Tears were running down my face."

He told his doctor that he spent upwards of $250 on one gram of heroin per day. So his doctor put him on a much higher dose of morphine than he would give to the average patient. "It was enough to take the edge off so that I wasn't lying there in tears, but I was still feeling the withdrawal." But when the shift changed, the next doctor cut his dosage to less than a quarter of that. Shawn was about to leave when the first doctor returned. "He flipped out. He said, 'What are you doing to my patient?'" Shawn was put back on the original dose.

Still, the nurses were often hours late with Shawn's next dose, which was already much lower than what he would take on the street. Against his doctors' advice, Shawn decided to leave the hospital after two weeks. He should have stayed on IV antibiotics, but health providers switched him to antibiotics in pill form. He got better initially, but now he has a swollen lump on his spine again. It's been agonizing for months, but, Shawn says, "I'm not going back to the hospital." He uses heroin to reduce the pain.

Shawn's experience isn't the exception. According to addictions specialists, patients often wait until their infection is unbearable and life-threatening before seeking treatment, due to past negative experiences. They tend to leave the hospital before they're fully healed, or even before they're treated at all, because they're forced to go into withdrawal or because they feel judged by health providers.

"Very vulnerable people aren't getting effective treatment," according to Jeff Turnbull, chief of staff at The Ottawa Hospital and medical director of the Inner City Health Project for the homeless in Ottawa. "That could lead to increased disability and even death."

Harm Reduction: The Standard of Care in the Community

For service providers in the community, expecting people to detox to access services is seen as a bygone approach. Earlier this month, for example, Toronto's city council approved three safe-injection sites, which were recommended by local boards of health. The sites have been shown to reduce the transmission of infectious diseases, like hepatitis C and HIV, and prevent deaths. The driving philosophy behind them – harm reduction – recognizes that, even with counselling and pharmaceutical therapy available, many people will continue to use drugs. The ultimate goal of harm reduction is for patients to stay alive and healthy enough to make it through what is usually a long, up-and-down struggle to recovery.

According to Ahmed Bayoumi, an internal medicine physician at St. Michael's Hospital in Toronto and an expert in health care for people who use drugs, it's time hospitals "accept that patients are going to use drugs" and start incorporating harm reduction strategies. A significant portion of people who are highly dependent on drugs or alcohol aren't ready to quit during the course of a hospital stay, he explains. "If someone is coming in for a complication that's related to their addiction, such as an infection, that usually means their addiction is pretty significant. And addiction is hard to treat," he says. "For us to take someone who is coming in for a completely different reason other than their addiction and expect them to suddenly be interested in having their addiction treated, that's pretty unrealistic." A common misconception is that even if someone isn't ready, a required, institutional detox can stop addiction in its tracks. That hardly ever happens, says Peter Selby, director of the addictions program at the Centre for Addiction and Mental Health in Toronto. In fact, forced detox in a prison or hospital dramatically increases one's risk of dying of an overdose in the week after release.

What Happens When Someone Who Uses IV Drugs Comes to the Hospital?

Typically, when someone shows up to the emergency department with track marks, or admits they've used opioids, they're labelled as "drug seeking" and aren't given painkillers. But once a patient is admitted, many hospital providers will give patients going through opioid withdrawal some level of the drug. Otherwise, "you're going to have a very sick patient on your hands," says Turnbull. Still, the dosages aren't usually enough to avoid withdrawal, says Turnbull, as providers worry about giving someone too much, and being held responsible for an overdose. "Someone might be taking a gram of morphine or using fentanyl, and a doctor in the hospital will give them maybe 10 mg of morphine. That's like taking a Smartie."

Of course, health providers need to know the severity of a person's addiction before they can offer long-term treatment or a temporary medical substitute. Given the stigma many patients with addictions face in health care, however, they don't often feel comfortable sharing how much or how often they use. And even if they do open up about their addiction, whether morphine or another replacement is offered depends on the provider and the hospital. "You might find a doctor who will help you out a bit, but then the next doctor or nurse has a completely different point of view in regards to harm reduction," says Sean LeBlanc, who was addicted to opioids for 10 years, and is now a peer support worker.

When LeBlanc himself was suffering from heroin addiction and had to get his tonsils out at a hospital, he was required to abstain. "I didn't need to be withdrawing from drugs at the same time as I was getting my tonsils out. Detoxing just makes the procedure so much worse," says Leblanc. He describes withdrawal like this: "Combine the worst flu with the worst hangover, and then add ten rounds of Mike Tyson."

[...]

> *"The facility's opening was linked to a 30 percent increase in detox use, which in turn was linked to pursuing long-term treatment and injecting at the facility less."*

Safe Injection Sites May Promote Uptake of Treatment

Chloe Reichel

In the following viewpoint, Chloe Reichel argues that, while hardly conclusive, research on the efficacy of safe injection sites shows promise. Safe injection sites, sanctioned spaces where people can use intravenous drugs safely under supervision, are illegal in the United States but have been used in Sydney and Vancouver. Preliminary research shows that clients using safe injection sites seem to be open to receiving treatment, based on their seeking treatment after referral. But US politicians are not convinced that safe injection sites are the answer to the country's growing opioid epidemic. Reichel is a research reporter for Journalist's Resource. Her work has also appeared in Cambridge Day, Cape Cod Times, *and* Harvard Magazine.

As you read, consider the following questions:

1. What is a safe injection site, according to the author?
2. What percentage of clients at the supervised injection site in Sydney went on to receive treatment after referral, as cited in the viewpoint?
3. What common concern surrounds safe injection sites as noted by the author?

M assachusetts Gov. Charlie Baker and Boston Mayor Marty Walsh have expressed skepticism over supervised injection sites as an effort to address the state's ongoing opioid epidemic. Baker suggested that the research on safe injection sites as a "path to treatment" was inconclusive.

Safe injection sites provide a space for people to use drugs intravenously with sterilized equipment and supervision to mitigate the dangers of overdose. Some also offer counseling, medical resources and referrals to treatment. While they are illegal in the U.S., a number of sites exist elsewhere, such as in Vancouver and Sydney.

Have these sites increased drug use or thwarted people who use drugs from seeking treatment? Or do they encourage users to enter treatment? Two reviews, one published in *Drug and Alcohol Dependence* in 2014, and one published in 2017 in Current HIV/ AIDS Reports, indicate that supervised consumption facilities promote uptake of treatment. The more recent review looked at 47 studies published between 2003 and 2017 on supervised drug consumption facilities. The authors found a handful of studies that demonstrated a positive link between safe injection site use and entry into treatment.

One of these studies compared detoxification enrollment among those who used Vancouver's supervised injection facility in the year before and after it opened. They found the facility's opening was linked to a 30 percent increase in detox use, which in turn was linked to pursuing long-term treatment and injecting at the

Substance Abuse and Racial Bias

Implicit bias among health care providers is a key factor contributing to racial and ethnic health disparities. Since implicit biases are automatic and subconscious associations that are expressed through attitudes and stereotypes, they can influence judgements and discriminatory behavior toward particular groups of people. This is dramatically apparent in treatment for drug and alcohol problems for people of color and in how our society repeatedly fails at providing treatment at potential points of intervention.

Individuals with drug and alcohol addiction encounter bias throughout their many points of contact within the criminal justice and health care systems, two of the main systems that serve as potential points for providing treatment. This bias is compounded when racial dynamics come into play, and we see these potential points of intervention turned into missed opportunities in a way that disproportionately affects people of color.

"Identifying Racial Bias in Treatment for Substance Use Disorders," by Ana Maria De La Rosa, Community Catalyst, September 19, 2016.

facility less. A later study of the site focused on use of detox services located at the facility, and found that 11.2 percent (147 people) used these services at least once over the two years studied. The authors conclude that these findings indicate supervised injection facilities might serve as a "point of access to detoxification services."

Another study of Vancouver's facility, published in the *New England Journal of Medicine* in 2006, found "an average of at least weekly use of the supervised injecting facility and any contact with the facility's addictions counselor were both independently associated with more rapid entry into a detoxification program." A 2011 study of the Vancouver facility published in Drug and Alcohol Dependence offered similar conclusions, and a qualitative account of injection drug users' experiences at the facility adds narrative backing to quantitatively documented benefits.

At a supervised injection site in Sydney, a year-and-a-half long study allowed researchers to determine that 16 percent of clients at the site referred to treatment went on to receive it, leading the authors to conclude that the center "engaged injecting drug users successfully in drug treatment referral and this was associated with presentation for drug treatment assessment and other health and psychosocial services." Reports from this site indicate that facility clients were more likely to start treatment than non-clients (38 percent vs. 21 percent).

Though supervised injection sites are illegal in the United States, one opened underground in 2014. The findings from the first two years of the site's operation were published in 2017 in the *American Journal of Preventive Medicine*. Each participant was asked the same set of questions about their use patterns every time they injected drugs at the site. From this data, the authors conclude that the site established a number of benefits, including safe disposal of equipment, unrushed injections and immediate response to overdoses. The authors add that if the site were sanctioned, it might be able to offer additional benefits, including healthcare and other services.

A concern around safe injection sites is that they increase drug use. But a study of 871 people who inject drugs found no substantial increase in rates of relapse into injected drug use among former users before and after the Vancouver site opened. However, the researchers also found no substantial decrease in the rate of stopping drug use among current users before and after the site opened. Another study of 1,065 people at this facility found that only one individual performed their first injection at the site, which counters fears that such facilities promulgate injection drug use.

Research indicates that many who use supervised injection facilities have the desire to access treatment. A study published in 2010 in the *Journal of Public Health* queried 889 people who were randomly selected at a supervised injection facility. "At each interview, ~20 percent of respondents reported trying but being unable to access any type of drug or alcohol treatment in the previous 6 months," the authors write. The main barrier to access, respondents said, was waiting lists for treatment.

Periodical and Internet Sources Bibliography

The following articles have been selected to supplement the diverse views presented in this chapter.

Dennis Cauchon, "Harm Reduction Success Story: Columbus' Needle Access Program," Harm Reduction Ohio, n.d., https://www.harmreductionohio.org/harm-reduction-success-story-columbus-needle-access-program/.

Anne Fletcher, "How Well Does Harm Reduction Work Over Time," Rehabs.com, October 3, 2016, https://www.rehabs.com/pro-talk-articles/how-well-does-harm-reduction-work-over-time/.

Futures Palm Beach, "Harm Reduction and Prevention," Futures Palm Beach, 2018, https://www.futuresofpalmbeach.com/addiction-research/harm-reduction-and-prevention/.

Harm Reduction Coalition, "Our Stories: Personal Testimonies," Harm Reduction Coalition, n.d., http://harmreduction.org/issues/syringe-access/overview/our-stories-personal-testimonies/.

Neil Hunt, "A Review of the Evidence-Base for Harm Reduction Approaches to Drug Use," Forward Thinking on Drugs, n.d., https://www.hri.global/files/2010/05/31/HIVTop50Documents11.pdf.

Institute for Behavior and Health, "Harm Reduction: An Approach That Is Damaging to Drug Users," Institute for Behavior and Health, n.d., https://www.ibhinc.org/harm-reduction/.

Andrea K. Knittel, Patricia A. Wren, and Lemont Gore, "Lessons Learned from a Peri-Urban Needle Exchange," Harm Reduction Journal, 2010, https://www.ncbi.nlm.nih.gov/pmc/articles/PMC2868839/.

Susan J. Rogers and Terry Ruefli, "Does Harm Reduction Programming Make a Difference in the Lives of Highly Marginalized, At-Risk Drug Users?," Harm Reduction Journal, 2004, https://www.ncbi.nlm.nih.gov/pmc/articles/PMC420490/.

Péter Sárosi, "Harm Reduction Beyond Numbers," Drug Reporter, November 12, 2017, https://drogriporter.hu/en/harm-reduction-beyond-numbers/.

Dan Wagener, "Harm Reduction," Drugabuse.com, 2018, https://drugabuse.com/library/harm-reduction/.

CHAPTER 2

Do Drug Users Have a Right to Quality Health Care?

Chapter Preface

For decades, US presidents and their administrations have sought to introduce programs to make healthcare benefits accessible and affordable for those in need. President Lyndon B. Johnson, for example, launched the Medicare system in 1965. However, as the population ages and as drug use continues to escalate, the 2010 Affordable Care Act, introduced by President Barack Obama, may seem inadequate. To opponents of the system, its essential benefits have resulted only in bottom line results for insurance, pharmaceutical, and medical supply companies while creeping out of the affordability range for many consumers.

Unlike other industrialized countries, the United States has not guaranteed universal health care as a right. Further, with each presidential administration, the system is either encouraged, threatened, or modified, causing strains on the population as well as criminal justice and other systems.

Harm reduction is one way to successfully manage recovery from addiction. If a network of healthcare centers in New York can effectively work with underinsured patients to create workable plans, other centers can, too. These plans "meet the patient where he or she is" by enabling patients to fill in their own attitudes, beliefs, and plans alongside the expert tips for recovery. In this way, patients own their own plans and take responsibility for their present and future conditions.

At the same time, though, drug users should be aware that their decisions affect family, friends, employers, coworkers, and everyone else around them. Their individual decisions can also impact the healthcare and criminal justice systems.

The following chapter analyzes whether drug users have a right to quality health care and identifies the conditions that either support or do not support it. The authors of these viewpoints put forth differing perspectives on a national healthcare system and what can be done even at local and state levels to help drug users with lower incomes get quality service and get past shame.

"Universal healthcare exists in every wealthy industrialized country on earth, except the United States."

Universal Healthcare Is a Right

Bernie Sanders

In the following viewpoint, Bernie Sanders argues for a universal healthcare system in America. He maintains that the current healthcare system only benefits healthcare companies. He calls for the reduction of Medicare eligibility to age fifty-five and reduced costs of prescription drugs. Sanders points out that America is the only highly industrialized country without universal healthcare and that it should be a guaranteed right as it is in many other countries. Sanders is a US Senator, who has been representing the state of Vermont since 2007. He ran for the Democratic presidential nomination in the 2016 election.

As you read, consider the following questions:

1. Which US president introduced Medicare?
2. What other industrialized countries guarantee universal healthcare?
3. Who are the real beneficiaries of the current healthcare system in America?

"Most Americans want universal healthcare. What are we waiting for?" by Bernie Sanders, Guardian News and Media Limited, August 14, 2017. Reprinted by permission.

As Americans, we need to answer some fundamental questions regarding the future of our healthcare system.

First, do we consider healthcare to be a right of all people, or a commodity made available based on income and wealth? Today, people in the highest-income counties in America live, on average, 20 years longer than people residing in the poorest counties. There are a number of reasons for that disgraceful reality, but one of them has to do with grossly unequal access to quality healthcare.

If you are upper-income and have good insurance, you go to the doctor on a regular basis, and life-threatening illnesses can be detected at an early stage when they can be effectively treated. If you are a working-class person without health insurance, or with high deductibles that keep you out of a doctor's office when you're sick, your chances of survival from a serious illness are significantly reduced.

In the wealthiest nation in the history of the world, should lower-income and working-class people have shorter and less healthy lives because they cannot afford the healthcare and medicine they need?

In my view, the moral answer is an emphatic No!

Second, why is our current healthcare system so enormously expensive? Today, despite having 28 million uninsured and even more under-insured, we are spending far, far more per capita than any other industrialized country – all of which guarantee healthcare to all of their people.

How does it happen that we spend almost $10,000 per capita each year on health care, while the Canadians spend $4,533, the Germans $5,353, the French $4,530, and the British $4,125?

Why, with that massive level of spending, is our life expectancy lower than most other industrialized countries, while our infant mortality rates are higher? Why do we pay, by far, the highest prices in the world for prescription drugs when nearly one out of five adult Americans cannot even afford the medicine their doctors prescribe?

Here is the simple truth: the function of our current healthcare system is not to provide quality, cost-effective care for all. Rather, it is to create a complicated, wasteful and bureaucratic system designed to make many hundreds of billions a year in profits for insurance companies, drug companies and medical equipment suppliers.

It is a system which makes CEOs and stockholders in the healthcare industry incredibly rich, while tens of millions of Americans suffer because they are unable to get the healthcare they need.

What can we do to better serve the American people?

In the short-term, with conservative Republicans controlling the White House, and both the Senate and the House of Representatives, we should fight to pass legislation which enables people in every state to select a public option, similar to Medicare, at affordable rates. This will provide competition among expensive private insurance plans and a choice in those areas where insurance companies have fled.

Further, we need to lower the Medicare eligibility to age 55. This would be a major relief for millions of older workers who, today, are unable to afford the skyrocketing premiums they are paying.

Lastly, we must take on the greed of the pharmaceutical industry and lower the cost of prescription drugs. There is no rational reason why pharmacists, distributors and individuals should not be able to safely import the same exact prescription drugs they use and sell today at far lower prices from Canada and other countries.

But even if these short-term fixes were made, it would still not be enough. The time is long overdue for a major overhaul of our health care system, one which creates universal, high quality and cost-effective healthcare for all.

I live in Burlington, Vermont, 50 miles south of the Canadian border. For decades, every man, woman and child in Canada has been guaranteed healthcare through a single-payer health care program. In fact, universal healthcare exists in every wealthy industrialized country on earth, except the United States. Germany,

France, the United Kingdom, Australia, Japan, Taiwan, and many others—all guarantee healthcare as a right. It's time we joined the rest of the industrialized world in that regard.

A half a century ago, the United States took a major step forward when President Lyndon Johnson signed legislation creating Medicare. Guaranteeing comprehensive health benefits to those over 65 has proven to be enormously successful and popular, and as a result, older Americans are living longer, healthier and happier lives. Now is the time to improve upon and expand Medicare, and make it available to every American – regardless of age.

Just as when Medicare was signed into law in 1965, there will be enormous opposition to the creation of a Medicare for All program from powerful special interests. The insurance companies, the pharmaceutical industry, the medical equipment manufacturers, Wall Street, and everyone else who profits off of our current system will spend hundreds of millions of dollars telling us how terrible that idea is, telling us that we can't accomplish what every other comparable country on earth has done.

But the American people know better. They want to go forward. An April 2017 poll from the Economist found that 60% of Americans, including 75% of Democrats, 58% of independents, and 46% of Republicans, support "expanding Medicare to provide health insurance to every American". Only 30% of those polled were opposed.

Establishing a Medicare for All single-payer program will improve the health of the American people and provide substantial financial savings for middle class families. It is the right thing to do. It is the moral thing to do.

Now is the time for us to summon the courage to create a healthcare system which benefits all Americans, and not just those who make billions off of the current wasteful, bureaucratic and dysfunctional system.

| "Opponents of the Affordable Care Act have long argued the essential health benefits rule has driven up the cost of insurance and health care."

The Affordable Care Act's Essential Health Benefits Are at Risk

Laura Santhanam

In the following viewpoint, Laura Santhanam argues that President Trump's new insurance proposal might put essential health benefits at risk. These essential benefits comprised a set of ten basics that all health insurance plans needed to carry. Santhanam points out, though, that these essential benefits have driven up the cost of healthcare. President Trump issued an executive order, carried out by the Department of Health and Human Services, to introduce short-term health plans. Santhanam is the Data Producer for the PBS NewsHour.

As you read, consider the following questions:

1. What are the ten essential healthcare benefits of the Affordable Care Act?
2. According to this viewpoint, is "Obamacare" threatened?
3. What do Affordable Care Act opponents believe the effect of the essential healthcare benefits have been?

Republicans in Congress may have failed to gut the Affordable Care Act last year, but that does not mean that Obamacare is safe.

For months, the Trump administration has been moving to weaken the law. This week, it released a proposal for "short-term" health care plans that would allow insurers to skirt many ACA requirements, including a mandate to offer essential health benefits. These are fundamental services, like maternity and newborn care and access to mental health and substance use disorder. Here's a look at why the 2010 law requires insurance companies to offer essential health benefits, and what losing them might mean for your insurance plan.

What Are Essential Health Benefits?

The goal of the Affordable Care Act was to give all Americans improved access to quality health care, while also reducing costs for consumers and the government. To strengthen health care, the ACA included these 10 essential health benefits to form a bare minimum of coverage that health insurance plans must have:

- Ambulatory patient services
- Emergency services
- Hospitalization
- Maternity and newborn care
- Mental health and substance use disorder services
- Prescription drugs
- Rehabilitative and habilitative services, along with devices
- Laboratory services
- Preventive and wellness services and chronic disease management
- Pediatric services, including oral and vision care

Why Did Obama and Democrats Push to Include Them in the 2010 Law?

The Obama administration and Democrats' argument for including essential benefits boiled down to three things, said Matthew Fiedler, who served as chief economist on the Council of Economic Advisers during the Obama administration:

- Avoid a race to the bottom in how we define health insurance.
- People who are healthy today likely don't know if they will become sick or injured tomorrow.
- Lifetime and annual caps on health care coverage added up to medical bankruptcy for many people.

"Having a baseline standard makes it easier for consumers to pick plans," said Fiedler, who is now a fellow at the Brookings Institution's Center for Health Policy.

Why Has the Trump Administration Proposed Changes to Essential Health Benefits?

Opponents of the Affordable Care Act have long argued the essential health benefits rule has driven up the cost of insurance and health care.

Republicans have also argued that essential health benefits force people to pay for services they do not need as individuals, such as who should pay for pregnancy. At a hearing last March, for example, Rep. John Shimkus, R-Ill., complained about what he deemed as unnecessary health care costs during a committee meeting: "What about men having to purchase prenatal care?"

Health insurance costs have risen, but with good reason, says Karen Pollitz, a senior fellow at Kaiser Family Foundation who studies health reform and private insurance.

"Health insurance that covers stuff will always cost more than health insurance that doesn't, just like a roller skate will always cost less than a car," she said.

Nevertheless, the Trump administration has used rising insurance costs to whittle away at the law after the GOP-controlled Congress failed to repeal Obamacare last year.

Last October, President Donald Trump signed an executive order that expanded short-term health plans, association health

Trump and the Nation's Health

At the same time, President Trump vowed to pull federal support from the subsidies that help people afford to purchase plans from the exchange.

As a result, premiums on ACA insurance exchanges may rise sharply, with negative consequences for public health. For example, women might find it more expensive to access prenatal and maternity care – something the US can in no way afford as maternal death rates are rising alarmingly. Amid a nationwide crisis of drug overdose that claimed more than 60,000 lives in 2016, coverage for substance use treatment may cost more.

The Trump administration should act to protect the right to health, not undermine it.

"Trump's Actions on Health Threaten Rights," by Megan McLemore, Human Rights Watch, October 16, 2017.

plans and health reimbursement arrangements, saying that "current regulations limit choice and competition."

People can now buy short-term limited duration health insurance plans for up to three months, a change the Obama administration put in place to discourage people from relying on these plans as health insurance.

These cheaper plans keep costs down by dropping any number of essential health benefits and rejecting applicants whose health care needs may be deemed too expensive to cover. The plans appeal to healthier people, but critics say they leave sicker people with costlier care in ACA-mandated health insurance risk pools where premiums then rise.

In his executive order last fall, Trump said he wanted to allow those plans to again offer just under 12 months of health insurance coverage. The Department of Health and Human Services released rules that would make those plans possible this week.

The Trump administration also gave states greater latitude to try new ways to change Obamacare, though those experiments are still panning out.

Thomas Miller, a resident fellow at the conservative American Enterprise Institute, said the order was an example of ways the Trump administration and new Health and Human Services Secretary Alex Azar could succeed in chipping away at Obamacare. Changing health care regulations will likely be easier than passing legislation, Miller said.

"They've got an improved team in with folks who know how to read regs and get something through without blowing it up," Miller said. "I think that will be further utilized, particularly in a difficult legislative environment."

What Happens Next?

Though HHS released new rules on short-term health plans this week, it's still not clear how essential health benefits may be at risk or what further action may be taken by the White House, federal agencies and states.

Fiedler said he is looking to the past to get a sense of what the future may hold.

"One can look back at the old individual market and look at the types of services not covered in plans," he said. "Various types of maternity services would probably be things that insurers would cut back on."

Miller said lifetime and annual caps appear to be safe, but bigger policy changes could be considered, including a move to develop a "megawaiver," combining waivers under section 1332 of the Affordable Care Act and section 115 under the Social Security Act. This could pool money that would act like a block-grant for health care for people with low income.

"If you put more money in the pot, you can close your eyes and think you're doing more," he said. "But you're really just moving furniture around."

> *"A network of health centers in New York state is using safety planning— which has most often been associated with reducing risk of suicide—in an attempt to reduce opioid overdoses."*

New York Health Centers Use Harm Reduction Safety Plans to Reduce Opioid Overdoses

Celia Vimont

In the following viewpoint, Celia Vimont argues that the use of two-page personalized Harm Reduction and Early Recovery Safety Plans have helped a network of twenty-six Institute for Family Health centers throughout New York effectively reduce the risk of opioid overdose among underinsured patients. These plans combine tips for recovery, yet give patients the opportunity to fill in their own reasons for and steps toward recovery. Celia Vimont is a writer for Partnership for Drug-Free Kids and is a freelance health and medical journalist. She received her master's degree in journalism from Columbia University in New York City.

As you read, consider the following questions:

1. What tool does the Institute for Family Health use to reduce the risk of opioid overdose?
2. Why is harm reduction an effective approach for the people at risk of overdose?
3. In what languages is the two-page safety plan available?

A network of health centers in New York state is using safety planning—which has most often been associated with reducing risk of suicide – in an attempt to reduce opioid overdoses.

The Institute for Family Health, which has community health centers throughout New York City and in the Mid-Hudson region, has designed and begun to use two-page, personalized Harm Reduction and Early Recovery Safety Plans, which take into account the different ways in which a person might be at risk of an opioid overdose.

"One group of people at risk of an opioid overdose are those who are actively using opioids, who may not be ready to stop," says Thomas McCarry, LMHC, Director of Substance Abuse Prevention at The Institute. "These people need a harm reduction approach, which acknowledges that not everyone wants to be free of substances, and even those who do may have a difficult time getting there. We tell them there are things they can do to take care of themselves and reduce possible health and other risks associated with using illicit drugs."

A second group of people have stopped using drugs. Some are intentionally working on recovery after treatment, while others may have stopped because they were incarcerated or are pregnant. They are still at increased risk of an overdose if they use opioids again, because they now have a lower tolerance than they did while they were still actively using drugs, McCarry says. These people need an early recovery safety plan focused on maintaining sobriety.

McCarry spoke about his organization's experience with implementing the new safety plans at the recent American Public Health Association annual meeting. The new safety plans are being used in all 26 health centers associated with The Institute, which are federally qualified health centers that are focused on serving underinsured patients. Once completed, the plans are stored in patients' electronic health records. They are available in English and Spanish.

"It is a tool for providers who may be less comfortable talking with patients about the risk of an overdose," McCarry says. "This is designed so that providers, regardless of their experience, can feel confident about having this conversation."

The harm reduction safety plan begins, "Though, we as your care team remain committed in the belief that everyone can recover, we also understand that not everyone chooses abstinence; even those who have sobriety as a goal often struggle to get there. And for some people, the current medications they are prescribed put them at increased risk of overdose."

The plan lists overdose prevention tips, including:

- Use less after any period of abstinence!
- Do not mix drugs, prescriptions, and/or alcohol.
- Use a less risky method (i.e. snort instead of smoke or inject)
- Test the strength of the drug before you do the whole amount.
- Do not use alone.
- Do not share or reuse needles.
- Develop an overdose plan with your friends or partner.
- Do not use when having thoughts of suicide.
- Keep a Naloxone "Narcan" Kit with you and learn how to use it.
- Seek medical attention after an overdose, even if you were given Narcan.

The plan leaves spaces for the patient to add ways they plan to reduce the risks associated with their drug use. At the end, it includes information about naloxone, and lists resources for getting help. It concludes, "Should abstinence or sobriety become your goal, please reach out for help and anyone on your care team can help you wherever you are on your path."

The personal recovery safety plan provides space for the patient to list their top reasons why they choose to be sober, and things they do regularly to stay sober. They also list actions they can take if and when they have cravings (such as call a support person, eating if hungry, going to a meeting, reading recovery material, reminding themselves that cravings can be intense but pass, or thinking of the consequences of using). They list places they can go that provide positive distraction (like 12-step meetings, a coffee shop, the library, or specific family or friends), their triggers or early warning signs (such as cravings, changes in attitude toward recovery, or behaviors), and space to list a few people they can call who support their recovery.

As with the harm reduction plan, it lists overdose prevention tips, recovery resources and information about naloxone. It concludes, "If you do have a slip, don't give up! Many people have had slips, so reach out for help and get back up. Good luck as your recovery journey continues!"

McCarry said he hopes the next step will be to research the effectiveness of these safety plans in reducing overdoses and deaths. "The two plans together show recovery is a circle, and not a straight line. Addiction is a chronic illness and relapse is something many people experience. We hope these tools will provide an integrated approach that addresses an individual's needs across all of their medical services, similar to those we use with other complex medical issues."

"Drug addiction is a complex illness with far reaching consequences for those who know, work with, and support the drug-addicted individual."

Drug Addiction Affects Everyone

DrugRehab.org

In the following viewpoint, experts at DrugRehab.org argue that drug addiction is a costly disease that affects the user, everyone around the user, and society on the whole. The organization's staff lays out the statistics of the number of abusers, the number of deaths from drug overdoses, and the costs of abuse. By using such statistics, DrugRehab.org maintains that a person's drug addiction affects families, friends, employers, and colleagues—in effect, society, in twelve ways. DrugRehab.org is a nationwide network of experts who provide state-by-state and 24/7 access to a broad range of services that includes residential treatment and detox.

As you read, consider the following questions:

1. Who are the hardest hit by an individual's drug addiction?
2. What are the twelve ways that drug addiction affects society?
3. On college campuses, what percentage of violent crimes involve the use of alcohol?

"How Does Drug Abuse Affect Society and You?" DrugRehab.org, January 2, 2015. Reprinted by permission.

Accroding to a recent study, nearly 24 million people in the United States abuse illicit drugs, nearly 18 million people abuse alcohol, and in 2012 alone 22,114 people died from prescription drug overdoses.

At any given time, approximately 10 percent of the US population is abusing drugs and alcohol, with multitudes of families, friends, neighbors, employers, and co-workers being directly affected. The costs associated with drug and alcohol use total nearly $600 billion in lost revenue, health care, legal fees, and damages each year. Drug abuse is associated with higher rates of foster care child placements, child abuse, college sexual assaults, prison sentences, and lost productivity coupled with increased work-related injuries.

Those who abuse drugs and alcohol are more likely to engage in risk-taking behaviors, have a higher co-occurrence of mental disorders, and are more likely to be incarcerated for crimes committed than non-drug using individuals. The burden in terms of costs, trauma, and influence on the nation's youth is substantial.

How Drug Abuse Impacts Families

Those closest to a drug-addicted individual are hardest hit. Common patterns emerge within families where at least one individual is addicted to drugs. These patterns include high levels of criticism or negativism within households, parental inconsistency, or in the case of parents coping with a drug-addicted child, denial. Misdirected anger between drug addicted and non-addicted family members is common as is self-medication as a strategy in coping with family dysfunction.

Co-dependent relationships often form between partners, where at least one partner is addicted to drugs and the majority of domestic disputes involve the use of alcohol or drugs. Children with one or more parents abusing drugs are more likely to take on the responsibility of the parental role, often functioning in denial of their parents' addiction or behaviors relating to the addiction. These children commonly lack basic necessities, including shelter, and have little to no health care. Similarly, families with at least one drug-addicted parent are more likely to end up homeless or in poverty, and are less likely to have adequate health care, representing a common barrier in obtaining treatment for the addiction.

Drug or alcohol abuse is the primary cause of more than 75 percent of all foster placements, and 80 percent of all child abuse and neglect cases cite drug or alcohol abuse as a primary factor. Rates of substance abuse among youth in foster care are significantly higher than comparative populations. Specific drug types are associated with higher rates of child custody losses. For example, fewer than 10 percent of babies born to untreated heroin addicted mothers reside their biological mothers at five years of age. And sadly, children of drug addicted individuals are eight times as likely to abuse drugs as adults.

Strain of Drug Addiction On Employers and Co-Workers

A 2006 study estimated that around 19 million people drink alcohol while at work, just before leaving for work, or go to work with hangover symptoms. This staggering number does not necessarily reflect daily abuse of alcohol at the workplace, but it does suggest a prevalence of accepted use of the intoxicant, despite known risks. Losses in revenue from decreased productivity due to illicit drug use in the workplace totals nearly $200 billion annually.

Co-workers of drug-addicted people take on additional responsibilities at work to accommodate decreases in productivity. They also work longer hours "covering for" drug addicted individuals who fail to show up as scheduled. Someone working while under the influence of drugs and alcohol is at higher risk of workplace related injury, resulting in increases in insurance premiums passed on to employers and co-workers.

A loss in productivity affects employers directly, and if drug-use is rampant, can result in loss of the business. Smaller to medium sized businesses are most at risk of failure resulting from drug related decreases in productivity. Estimates suggest working drug

THE WAR ON US

The war on drugs is a cruel joke. The U.S. spends more than $50 billion a year on the "war on drugs" with the goal of creating a "drug-free society" – yet there has never been a "drug-free society" in the history of civilization. Virtually all of us take drugs every single day. Caffeine, sugar, alcohol, marijuana, Prozac, Ritalin, opiates and nicotine are just some of the substances that Americans use on a regular basis.

The vast majority of Americans agree that the drug war is not working. So how should our society deal with people who use drugs? I propose three simple solutions: 1) Offer treatment and compassion to people who want help for their drug problems; 2) leave people alone who don't want or need treatment; and 3) continue to hold people responsible for crimes that harm others.

The war on drugs is really a war on us. It is time to stop arresting people simply for using or possessing drugs. Let's help people with drug problems, leave in peace those without a problem, and hold responsible those who harm others.

"How Should Our Society Deal with People Who Use Drugs?" by Tony Newman, Drug Policy Alliance, September 22, 2014.

users are a third less productive than their non-drug using co-workers.

Strain on Health Care System

Addiction is a chronic disease in this country. If you add up the annual accumulative costs of treatment for all brain-related diseases and double it; that's nearly the amount spent on addiction each year. Much of the money supporting the medical costs associated with drug addiction is absorbed by hospitals and taxpayers, with approximately 20 percent of Medicaid dollars and $1 in $4 Medicare dollars going to drug-addiction related expenses. The health care burden relating to drug abuse alone exceeds $180 billion annually.

Co-occurring mental disorders commonly precede or are the result of long term drug use and can increase costs associated with care. These costs are passed to the taxpayer and employer through higher insurance premiums and taxation. Coupled with a loss in productivity and lost wages, drug abuse represents an enormous financial burden on society and the economy.

Crime and Drug Addiction

Drug-related incarcerations make up more than 50 percent of federal prison populations and nearly 20 percent of state prison populations. Annual costs averaged across 50 states for state prison populations is greater than $32,000 per inmate, with federal stays averaging more than $26,000 per person, and the average drug-specific crime resulting in prison sentences of between three and nine years. Taxpayers shoulder the burden of $45 billion dollars for state prisons and $144 million for federal prisons annually.

The majority–approximately 80 percent–of incarcerated individuals has or is currently abusing illicit drugs or alcohol. Drug abuse is associated with substantial increases in rates of violent crime. Alcohol is a factor in 40 percent of the nearly 500,000 violent crime arrests made annually. Approximately a quarter of incarcerated individuals said their incarceration related directly to crimes committed to obtain money for drugs. On average, 5 percent of all homicides relate to drug use. Unfortunately, untreated, recidivism rates for drug use following prison release are as high as 95 percent.

On college campuses across the country, 95 percent of violent crimes reported, including sexual assaults, involve the use of alcohol. Violent crimes committed on college campuses can result in health care costs for the victims of these crimes, as well as lost revenue for universities.

How Drug Abuse Affects Society

- Increase in child custody losses
- Increase in child abuse and neglect
- Increase in addiction risks for children of drug-addicted parents
- Increase in domestic disputes

- Increased rates of homelessness and poverty
- Substantial financial health care burden
- Increased rates of co-occurring mental disorders
- Increase in insurance premiums, taxes
- Increased strain on co-workers
- Increase in number of people incarcerated in state and federal prisons
- Increase in rates of violent crimes on college campuses
- Losses in revenue for businesses and universities

Drug addiction is a complex illness with far reaching consequences for those who know, work with, and support the drug-addicted individual. Even if you don't know someone who is abusing drugs directly, you are likely impacted in other ways, whether through taxation, paying higher insurance premiums or college tuition, or in picking up hours at work. Drug addiction knows no boundaries.

Help for Drug Addiction Is Here

If you or someone you know is affected by drug addiction, DrugRehab.org offers online support and can connect you with professional support and treatment options to help you achieve recovery. Contact us and speak with someone today and take those first steps toward a new life free from and addiction to drugs and alcohol.

"*We saw diabetics who shared insulin syringes to save the expense of new ones. The substance being used doesn't matter—only the syringe.*"

Intravenous Drug Use Is a Public Health Issue

Jeannie D. DiClementi

In the following viewpoint, Jeannie D. DiClementi argues that needle exchange programs are an effective part of harm reduction treatment programs. The author focuses on syringe exchange efforts as a method of abating the rise of HIV in Indiana. She points out that intravenous drug users are injecting drugs for different reasons. The reality is there is a causal connection between shooting up and an upsurge in HIV, and efforts like syringe exchanges can help protect public safety. DiClementi is associate professor of psychology at Indiana University. Her research specialty is clinical health psychology.

As you read, consider the following questions:

1. Which former governor signed an exception to his state's restriction on needle exchange programs?
2. What percentage of HIV infections are caused by IDU?
3. What other benefits can needle exchange programs provide to intravenous drug users?

"Syringe Exchange in Southern Indiana to Respond to an Increase in HIV Cases: Better Late Than Never?" by Jeannie D. DiClementi, The Conversation, April 28, 2015. https://theconversation.com/syringe-exchange-in-southern-indiana-to-respond-to-an-increase-in-hiv-cases-better-late-than-never-40550. Licensed under CC BY-ND 4.0.

The recent upsurge in HIV cases linked to injection drug use in southern Indiana has thrust the issue of syringe exchange programs (SEPs) into the headlines. While authorities are linking these cases of HIV infection directly to injecting drugs, it is unknown how many are caused by sexual activity with an infected drug user.

Nearly all states prohibit possession of syringes other than for medical need through their drug paraphernalia laws. Syringe access laws that require ID and proof of medical need to purchase them from pharmacies also exist in the majority of states, including Indiana. Federal funding of syringe exchange programs is banned as well.

To respond to the current outbreak, Indiana Governor Mike Pence signed a 30-day exception to the state's restriction on needle exchange programs. The governor has extended the exception for another 30 days, as the state's legislature considers legalizing needle exchanges in some areas. The Centers for Disease Control and Prevention as well as other federal and state personnel are working to contain the outbreak.

This upsurge in HIV cases in Indiana hasn't exactly come out of nowhere. An increase in Hepatitis C cases (which can also be spread through re-used syringes) began nearly fifteen years ago in Scott County, so officials should not have been surprised that a corresponding rise in HIV cases would eventually follow.

Injection Drug Use and HIV

Injection drug use (IDU) is a well known risk factor for HIV, as well as Hepatitis B and C infections. The fact is that injection drug use accounts for about one-third of HIV infections in the country since the beginning of the epidemic.

Transmission of HIV occurs through an exchange of bodily fluids. In the case of injection drug use, transmission can occur not only by sharing needles, but by sharing any of the materials used to prepare and inject the drug, such as water or cotton used to filter the solution.

Women are particularly vulnerable, either from injecting drugs themselves, or from having unprotected sex with injection drug users, and women account for about twenty percent of new HIV infections yearly.

Why Do People Reuse Syringes?

In most states, access to syringes is severely restricted. This forces injection drug users to reuse or borrow syringes.

These laws intending to prevent illegal injection drug use, while perhaps well-intentioned, do not prevent it. Drug users do not quit because they don't have access to new syringes. Not having access to a clean glass doesn't keep me from being thirsty. Glass or no, I will find a way to get a drink of water.

Being forced to re-use dirty syringes places not only the drug user at risk of greater harm, but the public as well.

In my twenty years of work in the HIV field, I have seen patients who borrowed family members' insulin syringes, migrant workers who shared syringes used to inject liquid vitamins, hospital workers who recovered used syringes from the trash. These syringes are used repeatedly until the needle is too dull to pierce skin. One HIV-positive person places the entire needle-sharing network at risk.

For example, a 73-year-old grandmother was referred to our HIV clinic after her grandson, a 29-year-old addict, had infected her by using and returning her insulin syringes.

We saw groups of migrant workers who had shared needles to inject the liquid vitamins needed to withstand the hard labor, and who were all now HIV positive. We also saw diabetics who shared insulin syringes to save the expense of new ones. The substance being used doesn't matter – only the syringe.

Injection Drugs and Poverty: A Few Hours of Escape

Research also shows an association between poverty and both illegal drug use and HIV infection. The stresses of living in poverty are well known, and often people feel the only ways to relieve the stress include escaping through drug use.

In research conducted in 2011, at Indiana University-Purdue University Fort Wayne (IPFW), located in the center of northeast Indiana counties similar to Scott County, the epicenter of the latest outbreak, we interviewed fifty injection drug users about their drug use. Of the people we interviewed, only one was employed and the rest were living in impoverished situations. Some of the women survived by trading sex for drugs, others in the sample sold drugs – either illegal drugs or legal prescription medications.

They all agreed that getting high was one of the only times they felt good, and while they felt guilty about using drugs, they couldn't give up those few hours of escape that the drugs gave them. Becoming addicted, they then couldn't quit.

None of the people in our sample used drugs alone; they were accompanied by at least one other person, and everyone shared needles at least "several times." Frequent unprotected sex was reported, and only one person reported knowing their HIV status.

Frequently, as the CDC has reported for Scott County, families use drugs together, making it a multigenerational issue. In this case some cases also involve pregnant women who, in a resource-poor area, may or may not have access to treatments that would prevent transmission to their unborn child.

That isn't unusual. Many people with HIV don't know about their positive status. According to the Centers for Disease Control and Prevention, about 14% of 1.2 million HIV positive persons in the US do not know they are HIV positive.

Syringe Exchanges Can Also Provide Medical Services and Drug Treatment Information

Given the incidence of HIV infection in rural, impoverished areas, plus the transmission routes of shared injection syringes and unprotected sex, the situation in southern Indiana is not surprising, and a syringe exchange program (SEP) is a logical response. These programs have been around nearly as long as we have known how HIV is transmitted.

I worked with one such program. A typical SEP trades one sterile syringe for each used syringe. This approach does not put additional syringes on the street. Many programs also include bleach kits and instructions for properly cleaning syringes when clean ones are not available. They also provide condoms and information about safer sexual practices and includes the opportunity for HIV testing.

Research has consistently shown that SEPs do not increase drug use or the number of used syringes discarded in streets and playgrounds. Further, SEPs provide a point of contact for obtaining HIV testing, substance abuse counseling, screening for tuberculosis (TB), hepatitis B, hepatitis C, and other infections as well as referral for medical services.

When I handed out a sterile syringe, bleach kit, and condoms, I also included information about drug rehabilitation, jobs, housing, and my business card. More than once, I received phone calls months later from drug users I had contacted through the SEP who then wanted help with recovery.

Syringe Exchanges Should Be the Rule, Not the Exception

The response to the Scott County situation seems reasonable. However, given the predictability of this current outbreak based on the Hepatitis C increase beginning 15 years ago, the Scott County response comes late in the game.

Any HIV statistics are likely underestimates of the true numbers, and given the percentage of persons who are positive and do not know it, the incidence of known HIV cases in Scott and other Indiana counties is quite likely to increase.

Officials would have served the population better with preventative services in place. Governor Pence and the Indiana State Legislature would do well to put establishment of syringe exchange programs on a fast-track to-do list so there is a way to stem the tide of new HIV infections.

Periodical and Internet Sources Bibliography

The following articles have been selected to supplement the diverse views presented in this chapter.

American Addiction Centers, "Types of Health Care Coverage: Get the Help You Need," American Addiction Centers, 2018, https://americanaddictioncenters.org/insurance-coverage/.

Harm Reduction Coalition, "Quality Health Care Is Your Right: A Guide for Drug Users to Get Better Health Care," Harm Reduction Coalition, n.d., http://harmreduction.org/wp-content/uploads/2011/12/QualityHealthCare.pdf.

Karla Lopez and Deborah Reid, "Discrimination Against Patients with Substance Use Disorders Remains Prevalent and Harmful: The Case for 42 CFR Part 2," Health Affairs, April 13, 2017, https://www.healthaffairs.org/do/10.1377/hblog20170413.059618/full/.

Shatterproof, "Harm Reduction: Law and Policy," Shatterproof, n.d., https://www.shatterproof.org/harm-reduction-law-and-policy.

Substance Abuse Mental Health and Services Administration, "Treatments for Substance Abuse Disorders," SAMHSA, 2017, https://www.samhsa.gov/treatment/substance-use-disorders.

Cheryl Teruya, "Assessing the Quality of Care for Substance Use Disorder Conditions—Implications for the State of California," Addiction Technology Transfer Center Network, 2012, http://attcnetwork.org/regcenters/productDocs/11/Assessing%20the%20Quality%20of%20Care%20FINAL.pdf

Sarah Wakeman and Peter Friedmann, "Outdated Privacy Law Limits Effective Substance Use Disorder Treatment: The Case Against 42 CFR Part 2," Health Affairs, March 1, 2017, https://www.healthaffairs.org/do/10.1377/hblog20170301.058969/full/.

Emily Winkelstein, "Improving Health Care with Drug Users: Tools for Non-Clinical Providers, Curriculum Guide for Trainers," Health Reduction Coalition, n.d., http://harmreduction.org/wp-content/uploads/2012/02/ImprovingHealthCare-Facilitators-Guide.pdf.

Is Abstinence the Only Successful Method of Recovery?

Chapter Preface

The term "recovery" can mean different things to different people. While harm reduction and abstinence are often presented as two opposing ends of the substance addiction treatment spectrum, they may target different groups of users. Harm reduction can represent a fully comprehensive approach to reduce drug addiction. It takes motivation into account and engages in a lifestyle dialogue with the patient. It also maintains a drug-free society is impossible to achieve. It recognizes that not every patient seeks sobriety and that sobriety does not work for every patient.

Some viewpoints challenge the perception of harm reduction and abstinence as spectrum endpoints. They argue for building a bridge between them using either moderation management or a concept called gradualism. Most view recovery as a continuum of progressive steps with abstinence as the goal. However, some also point out that other issues typically accompany addiction and that recovery does not necessarily just mean cessation of use. There are often mental and behavioral issues involved that must be addressed and resolved for full recovery to occur. An imagined dialogue between Harm Reduction and Abstinence-Only concretely identifies the advantages and disadvantages of both approaches and concludes that rather than serving as opposite endpoints, they actually complement each other.

These viewpoints also present perspectives on other treatment strategies, including Alcoholics Anonymous. They question whether in abstinence-only programs substance dependence transfers to less life-threatening behaviors such as addiction to television or running.

The following chapter examines the efficacy of harm reduction and abstinence and proposes other approaches to bridge the two along a continuum. Statistics and the findings of other researchers help to build authors' arguments.

| *"A basic tenet of harm reduction is that there has never been, is not now, and never will be a drug-free society."*

Harm Reduction Takes a Comprehensive Approach to Reduce Drug Addiction

AlcoholAnswers.org

In the following viewpoint, specialists at AlcoholAnswers.org argue that harm reduction is based on three principles: (1) excessive behaviors occur along a risk continuum; (2) to change addictive behavior means taking it step by step with abstinence as the final step; and (3) sobriety isn't for everyone. They contend that harm reduction seeks to lessen harm through education, prevention, and treatment, and that harm reduction's goal is to restore basic human dignity to those suffering the disease of addiction. AlcoholAnswers.org is a website of the National Alliance of Advocates for Buprenorphine Treatment, a nonprofit organization formed in 2005 to help the public understand addiction as a disease, help reduce stigmas, and help connect patients with treatment providers.

As you read, consider the following questions:

1. Is there a single solution to bring about a drug-free society?
2. Does harm reduction, in general, believe a drug-free society is possible?
3. How is the success of a harm reduction strategy measured?

"Harm Reduction Philosophy," AlcoholAnswers.org. Reprinted by permission.

H arm reduction is a public health philosophy that seeks to lessen the dangers that drug misuse and our drug policies cause to society. A harm reduction strategy is a comprehensive approach to drug misuse and drug policy. Harm reduction's complexity lends to its misperception as a drug legalization tool.

Harm reduction rests on several basic assumptions. A basic tenet of harm reduction is that there has never been, is not now, and never will be a drug-free society. A harm reduction strategy seeks pragmatic solutions to the harms that drugs and drug policies cause. It has been said that harm reduction is not what's nice, it's what works. A harm reduction approach acknowledges that there is no ultimate solution to the problem of drugs in a free society, and that many different interventions may work. Those interventions should be based on science, compassion, health and human rights.

Problem drinkers vary considerably in terms of level of severity, configuration of antecedents which trigger heavy drinking, types of consequences which are of concern (e.g. legal, health, interpersonal) and individual goals and standards. Ideally, treatment for alcohol problems should begin with a thorough assessment of many variables so that a recommendation can be made as to the most potentially effective and least invasive approach which is most consistent with existing values. Some individuals can benefit from brief motivationally oriented contacts or involvement in self-help groups like Rational Recovery or Alcoholics Anonymous. Others require more intensive treatment, such as weekly individual therapy, partial hospitalization or inpatient treatment. Many individuals with drinking problems desire to learn how to moderate their drinking as opposed to abstaining. As stated, research strongly supports the efficacy of moderation training for non-physically dependent problem drinkers. Furthermore, many individuals who pursue moderation ultimately opt for an alcohol-free lifestyle. Moderation training, therefore, is appropriate and should be included in the spectrum of addiction treatments.

A person may have a problem with alcohol without being an alcoholic. According to recent data, most people only have mild to moderate alcohol problems. Relative to alcohol dependent individuals, these drinkers have a shorter problem drinking history, more social and economic stability, and greater personal resources. The first step is to make the drinker aware of the situations that trigger his or her drinking behavior when confronted with those situations. This cognitive-behavioral approach is designed specifically for problem drinkers who want to reduce their drinking and who do not have a strong physical dependence on alcohol.

The issue of controlled drinking still evokes violent debate. Most people don't know the facts regarding controlled drinking as a viable alternative for some problem drinkers. Popular press, driven by a strong 12-step coalition, has created an abstinence-only public mind set: Those with the disease of alcoholism (defined nebulously as "people with drinking problems") simply should not drink at all and that for professionals to advocate anything but abstinence and AA attendance is tantamount to malpractice.

Harm reduction approaches to addictive behavior are based on three central beliefs. First, excessive behaviors occur along a continuum of risk ranging from minimal to extreme. Addictive behaviors are not all-or-nothing phenomena. Though a drug or alcohol abstainer is at risk of less harm than a drug or alcohol user, a moderate drinker is causing less harm than a binge drinker. Second, changing addictive behavior is a stepwise process, complete abstinence being the final step. Those who embrace the harm reduction model believe that any movement in the direction of reduced harm, no matter how small, is positive in and of itself. Third, sobriety simply isn't for everybody. Bold and radical, this statement requires the acceptance that many people live in horrible circumstances. Some are able to cope without the use of drugs, and others use drugs as a primary means of coping. Until we are in a position to offer an alternative means of survival to these folks, we are in no position to cast moral judgment. It is held that the health and well-being of the individual is of primary concern; if individuals are unwilling or unable to change addictive behavior at this time, they should not be denied services. Attempts should be made to reduce the harm of their habits as much as possible.

A harm reduction strategy demands new outcome measurements. Whereas the success of current drug policies is primarily measured by the change in use rates, the success of a harm reduction strategy is measured by the change in rates of death, disease, crime and suffering. Because incarceration does little to reduce the harms that ever-present drugs cause to our society, a harm reduction approach favors treatment of drug addiction by health care professionals over incarceration in the penal system. A harm reduction strategy recognizes that some drugs, such as marijuana, are less harmful than others, such as cocaine and alcohol. Harm reduction mandates that the emphasis on intervention should be based on the relative harmfulness of the drug to society.

Harm reduction seeks to reduce the harms of drug policies dependent on an over-emphasis on interdiction, such as arrest, incarceration, establishment of a felony record, lack of treatment, lack of adequate information about drugs, the expansion of military source control intervention efforts in other countries, and intrusion on personal freedoms. Harm reduction also seeks to reduce the harms caused by an over-emphasis on prohibition, such as increased purity, black market adulterants, black market sale to minors, and black market crime. A harm reduction strategy seeks to protect youth from the dangers of drugs by offering factual, science-based drug education and eliminating youth's black market exposure to drugs. A harm reduction approach advocates lessening the harms of drugs through education, prevention, and treatment. Finally, harm reduction seeks to restore basic human dignity to dealing with the disease of addiction.

| *"Any form of treatment should reduce harm."*

A Dialogue Between Harm Reduction and Abstinence Only

Jana Burson

In the following viewpoint, Dr. Jana Burson argues both for and against the two ends of the addiction treatment spectrum, harm reduction and abstinence only. She fully imagines how advocates for each side would present their arguments in this balanced view. Yet, she recognizes abstinence as the ultimate in harm reduction and that harm reduction therapy, especially through methadone and buprenorphine, is effective. She concludes that harm reduction and abstinence only are no longer opposing strategies. Rather, they are complementary. Dr. Burson is a North Carolina medical doctor who specializes in treating patients with opioid addiction through methadone and buprenorphine.

As you read, consider the following questions:

1. Which professional agencies support harm reduction?
2. Which Medication-Assisted Treatment (MAT) has more supportive evidence, methadone or buprenorphine?
3. By the end of this dialogue, are Harm Reduction and Abstinence-Only still opposing each other?

I've heard the harm reduction versus abstinence -only debate about addiction treatment many times, not only at addiction medicine conferences, but also in my own head. In the past, I thought abstinence from all addictive drugs was the only true recovery from addiction. As I've aged, I've traveled far into the harm reduction camp, having seen people with addiction die from their disease when perhaps more could have been done to save them.

A wise mentor of mine once said try not to argue with people who aren't actually in the room with you, so I've committed the debate to writing.

Following is an imaginary debate between two addiction treatment professionals. One professional believes harm reduction measures are worthwhile because they can keep drug users alive and healthier, even if they never completely stop using drugs. The other professional feels harm reduction cheats a drug user out of full and happy recovery, which she believes is seen with complete abstinence from all drugs.

First, they chat about needle exchange:

HR: I fully support needle exchange programs. They have been proven to reduce transmission of infectious diseases, including HIV and hepatitis. Why wouldn't we want to help people avoid getting these potentially devastating diseases?

AO: Because giving out needles sends the wrong message. It says we are OK with people injecting drugs, and that we are willing to make it easier for them to do so. Appearing to condone drug use in any way sends the wrong message to young adults, who may be considering using drugs for the first time. Stigma towards drug users can be harmful, but perhaps stigma serves a good purpose if it discourages people from doing dangerous things like injection drug use.

HR: Studies do not show needle exchange increases the likelihood that people will start using drug intravenously. Easily available clean needles are not enough to convince a person to start injecting drugs. Besides, even if you have little compassion for the drug user, for every case of HIV we prevent with needle exchange, we save our society countless dollars in medical care. That's just one disease. When you consider the health burden and medical costs of transmission of hepatitis C, it's even more reasonable.

Even the ultra-conservative Mike Pence, the former Governor of Indiana and our future Vice President, changed his mind on needle exchange after an outbreak of HIV occurred in a rural community among people injecting opioids.

Besides being morally right, needle exchange makes financial sense.

AO: No, it doesn't. It sends a message to drug users that we've given up on them. It says we don't think they will ever be able to live without injecting drugs. In a way, it infantilizes them. By making drug use easier, we may cheat them out of trying to become clean and sober.

AO and HR move to the topic of medication-assisted treatment of opioid addiction with methadone and buprenorphine:

HR: First of all, medication-assisted treatment (MAT) is harm reduction only so far as all treatment should reduce harm. MAT is a good treatment in itself, and isn't necessarily just a stop on the journey of recovery.

I fully support medication-assisted treatment. We have fifty years of studies that show people who are addicted to opioids are less likely to die if they enroll in methadone maintenance or buprenorphine maintenance. It is one of the most heavily evidence-based treatments in all of medicine, and it is endorsed by many professional agencies, such as the Institute for Medicine, Substance Abuse and Mental Health Services Administration, the World Health Organization, and the American Society of Addiction Medicine.

We have study after study showing how opioid addicted people have a better quality of life when on medication-assisted treatment with methadone. We have more information about methadone because it has been use in the U.S. much longer than buprenorphine, which was approved by the Food and Drug Administration in 2002, after the Drug Addiction Treatment Act of 2000 was passed.

Opioid-addicted people enrolled in methadone treatment are more likely to become employed, much less likely to commit crime, and more likely to have improved mental and physical health. They receive addiction counseling as part of the process of treatment.

We think buprenorphine has the same benefits, though there have been fewer studies than with methadone. We do know the risk of opioid overdose death is much lower when an opioid addicted person is treatment with buprenorphine, too.

Because medication-assisted treatment is so effective, it should be considered a primary treatment of opioid addiction, and not only a harm reduction strategy.

AO: With MAT, opioid-addicted people may be harmed more than if they continue in active addiction. It is no different from giving an alcoholic whiskey. Methadone is a heavy opioid that's difficult to get off of. The opioid treatment programs that administer methadone don't try to help these people to get off of methadone, because they make more money by keeping them in treatment. These patients are chained to methadone with liquid handcuffs forever. It's also expensive over the long run, and patients have to agree to many restrictions put on them by state and federal governments.

HM: Methadone and buprenorphine treatments are not like giving an alcoholic whiskey, because the unique pharmacology of these medications. Both medications have a long half-life, and when patients are on a stable dose, they feel normal all day long without cravings for illicit opioids. This frees them from the unending search for drugs that occupies much of their days. Instead, they can concentrate on positive life goals.

Also, even after an opioid- addicted person stops using opioids and endures the acute withdrawal, he will usually feel post-acute withdrawal. This syndrome, often abbreviated PAWS, can cause fatigue, body aches, depression, anxiety, and insomnia. It's unpleasant. Many people in this situation crave opioids intensely.

We think this occurs because that person's body no longer makes the body's own opioids, called endorphins.

Endorphins give us a sense of well-being, and without them, we don't feel so good. When humans use opioids in any form, our bodies stop making endorphins. In some people, it takes a very long time for that function to return. In some cases, it may never return. We can't yet measure endorphin levels in humans, so this is a just theory, but one borne out by years of observation and experience.

Methadone and buprenorphine are both very long-acting opioids. Instead of the cycle of euphoria and withdrawal seen with short-acting opioids, these medications occupy opioid receptors for more than twenty-four hours. It can be dosed once per day and at the proper dose, it eliminates craving for opioids, and eliminates the post-acute withdrawal, which is so difficult to tolerate.

We often compare opioid addiction to diabetes, because in both cases, we can prescribe medication to replace what the body should be making.

And yes, methadone is difficult to taper off of, but most of the time it is in the patient's best interests to stay on this medication, rather than risk a potentially fatal relapse to active opioid addiction. Some patients are able to taper off of it, if they can do it slowly.

Do you think of a diabetic who needs insulin as being "handcuffed" to it? Do you think the doctor who continues to prescribe insulin is just trying to make money off that patient? Why is it wrong to make money from treating addiction, but not other chronic diseases?

AO: What about all of the former opioid-addicted people, now in 12-step recovery, who are healthy and happy off all opioids? Why are these people doing so well, even though they had as severe an addiction to opioids as the patients in opioid treatment programs?

HR: We don't have all the answers to this question. One form of treatment, even medication-assisted treatment, won't be right for every patient. Maybe the support that a 12-step group can provide got these people through the post-acute withdrawal. We don't have much information about these recovering people, obviously due to the anonymous nature of that program.

If these people feel OK off all opioids, that's great. They don't need medication. But don't prevent other people who do benefit from medication-assisted treatment to be helped with methadone, and buprenorphine.

Besides, not all opioid-addicted people want to go to 12-step meetings. Do treatment professionals have the right to insist everyone go to these meetings, even if patients don't like them?

AO: Medications cheat patients out of full abstinent recovery. Methadone and buprenorphine blunt human emotions, and make it impossible to make the spiritual changes necessary for real recovery. Methadone and buprenorphine are intoxicants, and they prevent people from achieving the spiritual growth needed for full recovery. You keep these people from finding true recovery, and condemn them to a life of cloudy thinking from these medications.

HR: Various people assert patients on maintenance methadone and buprenorphine have blunted emotions and spirituality, but there's no evidence to support that claim. How can you measure spirituality? If spirituality means becoming re-connected with friends and loved ones and being a working, productive member of society, then studies show that methadone and buprenorphine are more likely.to assist patients to make those changes.

Physically, studies show patients on maintenance methadone and buprenorphine have normal reflexes, and normal judgment. They are able to think without problems, due to the tolerance that has built up to opioids. They can drive and operate machinery safely, without limits on their activities. Contrary to popular public opinion, patients on stable methadone doses are able to drive without impairment.

However, if that patient mixes drugs like sedatives or alcohol with methadone, they certainly can be impaired. That's why patients should not to take other sedating drugs with medication-assisted treatments.

People with opioid use disorder are far more likely to make significant and healthy life changes if they feel normal, as they do on medications like methadone and buprenorphine. If they chose abstinence, many times they feel a low-grade withdrawal for weeks or months, and this makes going to meetings and meeting life's responsibilities more difficult.

Remember: dead addicts can't recover. Far too many opioid-addicted people have abstinence-only addiction treatments rammed down their throats. Most of these patients aren't even told about the option of medication-assisted treatment, which is much more likely to keep an opioid drug user alive than other treatment modalities.

Too often, people addicted to opioids cycle in and out of detoxification facilities over and over, even though we have forty years of evidence that shows relapse rates of over 90% after a several weeks' admission to a detox facility. We've known this since the 1950's, and yet we keep recommending this same treatment that has a low chance of working. And then we blame the addict if he relapses, when in reality he was never given a treatment with a decent chance of working!

Medical professionals, the wealthy, and famous people are treated with three to six months of inpatient residential treatment, and they do have higher success rates, but who will pay for an average opioid user to get this kind of treatment? Many have no insurance, or insurance that will only pay for a few weeks of treatment. For those people, medication-assisted treatment can be a life-saving godsend. It isn't right for every opioid-addicted person, but we do know these people are less likely to die when started in medication-assisted treatment. After these people make progress in counseling, there may come a time when it is reasonable to start a slow taper to get off either methadone or buprenorphine, but first we should focus on preventing deaths.

AO: Given the time, money, expense, and stigma against methadone and buprenorphine, it should be saved as a last resort treatment. If an opioid-addicted person fails to do well after an inpatient residential treatment episode, then MAT could be considered as a second-line treatment. Let's save such burdensome treatments for the relapse-prone opioid-addicted people.

HR: It seems disingenuous to claim stigma as a reason to avoid MAT when you are the one placing stigma on this treatment.

I could go on for many more pages, so let's stop here. You get the idea.

In the past, harm reduction and abstinence were considered opposing views. I've heard some very smart people say this is a false dichotomy, and that in real life, these views are complementary.

I like this newer viewpoint.

Any form of treatment should reduce harm. If a patient achieves abstinence from drugs, then that's the ultimate reduction of harm. Also, harm reduction principles can help keep drug users alive, giving them the opportunity to change drug use patterns later in life. As I've said above, dead addicts don't recover. Let's give people more choice and more opportunities to transition out of drug use, if that's what they desire.

VIEWPOINT

> *"Recovery always includes some form of harm reduction, in the fullest sense of that term."*

Recovery Is a Continuum

Julia Hammid

In the following viewpoint, Julia Hammid argues that abstinence and recovery are not the same thing. Recovery can actually be defined in a variety of ways, and each one of these involves some form of harm reduction. She points out that even advocates of abstinence find they transfer a dependence onto something else, for example, members of Alcoholics Anonymous becoming addicted to the coffee and donuts. Hammid herself suffered from bulimia some fifteen years ago and came to understand that her recovery included steps of harm reduction. Hammid is a guest writer for neuroscientist Marc Lewis' blog Understanding Addiction. She is a community mediator in Maryland.

As you read, consider the following questions:

1. What will exist no matter what we say?
2. Is Alcoholics Anonymous a form of harm reduction?
3. Are there other issues to be addressed if recovery is achieved?

"Harm reduction vs. abstinence?" by Julia Hammid, From "Understanding Addiction" blog by Marc Lewis (http://www.memoirsofanaddictedbrain.com/blog/), February 21, 2014. Reprinted by permission.

J udging by the volume and intensity of the discussion around Harm Reduction (HR), both here and in many other venues, it seems to be a flashpoint for identifying some of the core issues driving policy, research and personal opinion in regards to addiction (even as the term addiction is still being defined). In the spirit of promoting an illuminating and productive conversation around addiction, recovery and treatment, here are some of my thoughts on HR. Just for the record, I am in favor of HR as a concept, though I may not agree with every version of how it's provided.

So, why the brouhaha around HR? Doesn't it just describe a broad variety of strategies to counteract the damage of addiction, short of complete abstinence? The question is not so much whether HR should exist. It's going to exist no matter what we say. The question is whether or not we like it and support it. For example, we dispute whether the powers that be should fund programs that provide clean syringes, safe spaces to use, and even the (uncontaminated) substances themselves. In my mind, HR includes a lot more. In fact, I would claim that most, if not all, recovery includes some form of HR, even if complete abstinence is the goal.

While addiction includes a vast array of substances and behaviors, abstinence can only be applied to selected substances, mostly illegal ones. How are we to define abstinence from addictions that are not measurable with a blood test? And even where abstinence is the only goal, where HR is most controversial, those who are abstinent from the identified substance often end up substituting or relying on (dare I say becoming addicted to?) other substances or behaviors, which fly under the radar. For instance, there's a joke around AA about being addicted to the donuts and coffee that are ubiquitous at meetings.

I am not saying that addiction cannot be overcome or that one thing is always replaced by another or that any of the above is bad. I am just saying that I think, with few exceptions, recovery is always a continuum and always includes some form of HR, in the fullest sense of that term. More often than not, there is a period of shifting of dependence from the target bad thing to other less harmful (or simply legal and more easily obtained) things. Even seemingly positive things can be pursued with some of the same desperation that the original addiction carried, including socially approved addictions such as, coffee, sugar, TV, running, the internet, or even "dependence" on therapeutic treatment, religion, etc. I know some people who are so immersed in their 12-step community that their whole lives revolve around meetings, the literature and the people they know in that community. I'm not saying that's a bad thing. I'm just saying that it should be recognized as a form of HR.

To some, HR connotes state-supported addiction. But that is nothing like the actual goals of HR proponents. The controversy is kept alive by discrepancies such as these. In contrast, I think the word "abstinence" carries its own social and psychological baggage and may misrepresent what the opponents of HR are arguing for. Abstinence is not a term I personally find appealing. For me it connotes ascetic monks trying to rise above earthly existence by denying themselves much of what makes life worth living. Abstinence puts the focus on what one is not doing, rather than looking forward to what is truly worthwhile. In some ways, full blown addicts are abstinent from life, foregoing all its richness in pursuit of their addiction. Most agree that abstinence from a particular drug or behavior is far more precious.

A story was shared in response to a post on this blog, about a relative being instructed to just apply a cool cloth to the addict's forehead and in a few weeks they would "be good as new." As any recovering addict will tell you, it takes a lot more! And much of what it does take I would classify as HR. Even if you quit the identified addiction, there are still a mountain of other issues that need to be addressed, such as recovery from the trauma that may have been driving the addiction, employment, reputation, how to create/repair a life, a family, a community. From the addict's point of view, support for those tasks is as essential as stopping using. And much of that work can begin while engaging in "official" HR services.

Society sees addiction as a drain on its resources (unproductive individuals sucking up services) and a source of harm to others (crime, disease, embarrassment, etc.). So, from society's perspective, fully abstaining from the addiction removes all the above negative consequences. But from the perspective of addicts (and those who are able to step into their shoes, whether family or treatment providers) it's not at all that simple.

Abstinence and recovery are not one and the same. As opposed to simply stopping using the target substance, "complete" recovery is as varied as are humans. Life is, by its very nature, imperfect, and applying definitions of things such as addiction, abstinence, sobriety, and recovery to real people will always be approximate.

The core arguments I'm hearing are about who pays for what services and strategies, what the authorities endorse, and what is socially and ethically acceptable. We can, and should, argue about specific programs, policies and laws, but trying to agree on one "correct" way to recover from addiction ignores the valiant struggles and triumphs of so many who have recovered, one way or the other. I was bulimic for over 15 years (many years ago), which was as intractable, self-abusive and life threatening as addiction to any drug. And I am quite certain it would have killed me had I continued. As with other less clear-cut addictions, recovery for me is a continuum, one which involved plenty of what I would certainly call Harm Reduction.

> "While it may sound like a bit of an oxymoron, some believe that addicts and substance abusers can achieve sobriety while still drinking alcohol or using drugs on occasion."

Using Moderation Management to Control Substance Addiction

DualDiagnosis.org

In the following viewpoint, DualDiagnosis.org specialists argue for controlling drug and alcohol addiction through a variety of methods, including moderation management, self-discovery and recovery training, harm reduction, Alcoholics Anonymous, and others. They conclude that moderation management has the best rate of success. DualDiagnosis.org is a website of the Foundations Recovery Network, founded in 1995. The organization serves people with a dual diagnosis of substance addiction and mental health disorder. It offers outpatient services, vocational rehabilitation, and residential programs in Malibu, California, Palm Springs, California, and Memphis, Tennessee.

As you read, consider the following questions:

1. What is moderation management?
2. What statistics point to abstinence as being successful or unsuccessful?
3. Who founded the Moderation Management organization?

"Recovery: Abstinence vs. Moderation," DualDiagnosis.org. Reprinted by permission.

Typically, the first thing that comes to mind when thinking about addiction recovery is how to quit using or abusing a substance forever. There are proponents of another theory though, that one can control addiction through moderation management (MM) behaviors, and there is evidence to support this theory, too.

Abstinence

Abstaining is the most traditional treatment method surrounding drug and alcohol abuse. This method involves completely avoiding substance use and abuse. While abstinence has long been held as the only way to resolve an addiction problem, and it may be highly effective when achieved, actually reaching the goal of abstinence seems to be the biggest problem.

A Scottish study of 695 participants carried out in 2006 reported just a mere 5.9 percent of females and 9 percent of males as having been completely abstinent for at least 90 days prior to the interview 33 months after recruitment.[1]

Abstinence is an effective method of treatment when maintained. Among individuals who remain abstinent for one to three years, only around 34 percent will end up relapsing. This number drops to 14 percent among those who manage to remain abstinent for five years.[2]

Those who are seeking abstinence will be most likely to reach this goal through professional treatment. Past-year data from 2012 supports long-term abstinence as possible and more likely if the addict has sought treatment at some point. The data reflects 56.1 percent of individuals who had begun to engage in alcohol abuse 20 or more years prior and sought treatment at some point were abstinent, compared to 24.5 percent who were never treated being abstinent.[3]

Similar data for heroin, cocaine and amphetamine abusers showed that at least 27 percent of the 899 participants one study began with were no longer living 20 years later, and among them, just 27 percent were abstinent from the aforementioned drugs and methadone for at least four months since they initiated such drug use 20 years before.[4]

Moderation Management

Believe it or not, abstinence isn't the only path people try to take to sobriety. While it may sound like a bit of an oxymoron, some believe that addicts and substance abusers can achieve sobriety while still drinking alcohol or using drugs on occasion. The theory behind this is that it may work best for those substance abusers who are not physically dependent on drugs or alcohol and who have suffered few negative side effects from their substance abuse behaviors, such as delirium tremens or substance cravings.

This theory supposes that the common alcoholic — something 17.7 million people were classified as in 2012[5] — can manage their addiction by limiting how much and how often they drink.

When it comes to drug abusers, the theory carries less weight. While a single episode of binge drinking can lead to death — of the 38 million admitted binge drinkers, there were 2,200 deaths due to alcohol poisoning[6] — it's far more likely that a person would die from a single use of hard, illicit substances like heroin. In 2013, 8,260 people died following the use of heroin in the United States.[7] Thus, moderation management can be dangerous when used to end certain drug habits.

Only 2.5 million of the 23.1 million people in America who needed treatment for a substance abuse problem got it in 2012. [8] Many addicts claim the reason they don't pursue treatment is due to not feeling like they're ready to stop using — combined data from 2010 to 2013 shows that 24.5 percent of the millions of individuals who needed treatment but didn't get it reported this being the reason why.[9] Among problem drinkers, nine out of 10 resist seeking traditional treatment on purpose.[10]

But moderation in recovery is not advised by many in the treatment community. Over the years, treatment views toward substance abuse have changed, even in the eyes of treatment providers. In 1994, around 25 percent of the 913 counselors interviewed claimed that an occasional drink was okay for alcohol abusers who wanted to decrease how much they drink without totally quitting; that figure has risen to 50 percent as of 2012.[11] In one study focused on the duration of abstinence rates among 1,222 participants, only just 418 of them achieved abstinence for a year or longer following treatment.[12]

The Moderation Management organization came along in 1994 as a controversial counterpart to the more traditional and abstinence-minded Alcoholics Anonymous. Its founder, Audrey Kishline, felt her alcohol use was a problem, but not so much that she thought of it as a disease or chronic illness. Although she would later end up confessing openly that moderation didn't work out for her, she still fully supported it as an option for others, and since then many have jumped on board and made successful turnarounds in their lives with the MM program.

In the program, accountability is high on the list of must-haves, and an online, interactive calendar where MM members can report their drinking or drug use keeps them on track with their pattern of substance use and holds them responsible for it. Members can take advantage of in-person meetings, just like AA offers, or opt for online encounters that serve the same purpose while providing more flexibility. The program's website offers detailed guides on how much alcohol use is permissible and message boards where members can discuss their struggles and find praise for their achievements.

The program encourages you to focus on your substance abuse patterns. When do you use? Why? Those are important questions, because their answers reveal wounds that need fixing and a general lack of coping skills. When these issues are repaired, the urge to drink when upset or as a way to avoid emotions may be managed.

Other Methods

The program operates virtually so that members remain truly anonymous, and lifetime membership isn't a requirement. Labels of addiction aren't a part of this program, because there is no shame involved. Absent of religious affiliation, SMART Recovery teaches members the tools they need to practically handle their substance abuse problems without a commitment to a higher power, but more so with a commitment to themselves. The program is most popular with alcohol abusers, but isn't solely aligned with them.

A UK review of participants tallied 67 percent of surveyed members sought out the program for their drinking, while 36 percent did for an opiate addiction, 10 percent for a marijuana or stimulant dependency, and seven percent for other drugs, with 19 percent of respondents reporting poly-substance abuse.[13]

Abstinence and MM aren't the only remedies for alcohol abuse. Self-Management and Recovery Training (SMART Recovery) is another treatment option that concentrates on four main principles, which are:

- Creating and sustaining motivation
- Managing urges to use
- Controlling thoughts, emotions, and actions
- Living a well-rounded life

Rational Recovery, which centers on a singular approach to recovery with no support groups or regular meetings to attend, utilizes the Addictive Voice Recognition Technique. In other words, the idea is that you are constantly battling a beast inside yourself that wants to lure you back to substance abuse. The program allows participants to consider themselves fully recovered on day one and to operate with that mindset moving forward.

Today, there is a strong push for help on the pharmaceutical front that can assist some problem drinkers in curbing their alcohol abuse. Naltrexone has aided in inhibiting the desired high many drinkers receive from alcohol abuse, and thus, it makes many lose the desire to seek it. Others have benefitted from Antabuse, a commonly prescribed drug that induces vomiting when mixed with alcohol.

Opioid antagonist nalmefene has been approved for opioid overdose treatment in the US, but not yet for alcohol abuse as it has elsewhere. Still, it may be a promising movement in the future. A manufacturer study touted impressive results among 604 participants that decreased the number of days they drank heavily from 19 to eight over six months' time and lowered their overall rate of alcohol use by about two-thirds.[14] Essentially, the drug curbs the drinker's craving to go beyond the consumption of a couple drinks at happy hour.

One program known as Harm Reduction, Abstinence, and Moderation Support (HAMS) focuses more on the lifestyle-related causes of drug and alcohol abuse. It recognizes the frequency with which these behaviors are tied to social activities and aims to assist members in reaching self-set goals. Some of these individuals may seek to stop drinking altogether. Others might just want to scale things back, while some may be seeking ways to continue engaging in the substance abuse habits they choose while learning how to make those practices safer and less likely to cause harmful side effects.

HAMS strongly urges members to pay attention to how they feel before, during, and after drinking or using drugs. These revelations can come in handy afterward. For example, a problem drinker may feel great after two or three drinks, thus encouraging him to keep going, but he finds through the HAMS program that after four or five, he begins to feel sad and depressed. Those negative emotions then drive him to keep drinking, and he may learn through this experience that two or three drinks needs to be his limit.

Criticism

Critics of Alcoholics Anonymous — the largest abstinence-based program in existence — continue to say that AA boasts poor success rates, just five to 10 percent among some sources, though the organization states that success rates can't be measured correctly due to the anonymous nature of the group.[15] There are also drawbacks to moderation management, and those who are against it have concerns that aren't unfounded.

Some people aren't fans of the modernized method and tout moderation as nothing more than an excuse to relapse. The biggest risk involved in moderation management is staying accountable. It isn't uncommon for those practicing the MM method to hide their excess drinking or use their participation in the program as an excuse to drink more than they should be. It often aids in staving off concerns from others in their life, too. Of course, while critics of MM are quick to point out the potential for falsely subscribing to program practices, the same can be said of abstainers. Personal accountability is a big part of MM, just as it is with AA.

Some worry that moderation practices may encourage alcohol use among abusers, seeing drinking in moderation as a free pass to continue abusing alcohol when it has been an obvious problem in the abuser's life. Proponents of the MM program feel this is not true. Those individuals who cannot maintain moderation habits in the MM program generally end up moving on to abstinence programs, something a reported 30 percent of MM participants do.[16]

Other critics have concerns that the MM program will give abstinent substance abusers the idea that they can return to using and keep it under control. Supporters say that the program doesn't entice relapse, and those who have such ideas about MM generally would have relapsed anyway.

The focus of moderation management is not to deter substance abusers from abstinence or draw them away from an already present commitment to such. Rather, there is more concern in the substance abuse treatment community over the number of addicts who never even attempt to seek treatment — a figure that accounts for around 90 percent of the substance-abusing population.[17] The moderation management protocol may serve as a feasible way for many of those individuals to seek help or at least be more inclined to. Likewise, MM acts as a gateway to abstinence later on for a large number of participants.

Still, many who are in favor of abstinence will tell you that problem drinkers generally have one thing in common — they drink too much and cannot control it. So they pose the question: How then will they learn to do just that — control their drinking habits? Whether the outcome of a childhood experiences or causing a ruckus in college, binge drinking and drug experimentation are often part of the young American's culture. As of 2005, 68 percent of a sample of American college students were drinkers and 40 percent of them admitted to binge drinking.[18]

In a study of 90 heavy drinkers that participated in MM and were monitored at three, six and 12 month intervals following such, those who utilized the MM website were able to increase their rate of monthly alcohol management from 16 percent to 20 percent — results that persisted throughout the entire study period.[19] In addition, they decreased their blood alcohol content levels by half, even on days they were drinking.[20] Those who utilized the MM interactive site were able to reach a 40 percent rate of abstinence throughout the month.[21]

Notes

[1] McKeganey, N., Bloor, M., Robertson, M., Neale, J. & MacDougall, J. (2006). "Abstinence and drug abuse treatment: Results from the Drug Outcome Research in Scotland study." Informa Healthcare. Accessed May 14, 2015.

[2] "Extended abstinence is predictive of sustained recovery." (July 2008). National Institute on Drug Abuse. Accessed May 14, 2015.

[3] "Substance Recovery Rates: With and Without Treatment." (2012). The Clean Slate. Accessed May 14, 2015.

[4] Termorshuizen, F., Krol, A., Prins, M. & Van Ameijden, E.J.C. (2005). "Long-term Outcome of Chronic Drug Use." American Journal of Epidemiology. Accessed May 14, 2015.

[5] "DrugFacts: Nationwide Trends." (January 2014). National Institute on Drug Abuse. Accessed May 14, 2015.

[6] "Alcohol Poisoning Deaths" (2015). Centers for Disease Control and Prevention. Accessed May 14, 2015.

[7] Kounang, N. (2015 January 14). "Heroin deaths up for 3rd year in a row." CNN News. Accessed May 14, 2015.

[8] "DrugFacts: Nationwide Trends." (January 2014). National Institute on Drug Abuse. Accessed May 14, 2015.

[9] "Substance Use and Mental Health Estimates from the 2013 National Survey on Drug Use and Health: Overview of Findings." (2014 September 4). Substance Abuse and Mental Health Services Administration. Accessed May 14, 2015.

[10] "Why is a Moderation Program Needed?" (n.d.). Moderation.org. Accessed May 14, 2015.

[11] Davis, A. & Rosenberg, H. (2012 November 2). "Study: Alcohol, Drug Abuse Counselors Don't Always Require Total Abstinence." American Psychological Association. Accessed May 14, 2015.

[12] Scott, C.K., Dennis, M.L., Laudet, A., Funk, R.R. & Simeone, R.S. (April 2011). "Surviving Drug Addiction: The Effect of Treatment and Abstinence on Mortality." American Journal of Public Health. Accessed May 14, 2015.

[13] Bitel, M. (January 2014). "The evaluation of SMART Recovery in the Lothians." SMART Recovery UK. Accessed May 14, 2015.

[14] Andrey-Smith, P. (2014 October 19). "A Pill Could Help Alcoholics, and Let Them Drink in Moderation." Newsweek. Accessed May 14, 2015.

[15] Dodes, L. & Dodes, Z. (2014 March 23). "The pseudo-science of Alcoholics Anonymous: There's a better way to treat addiction." Salon. Accessed May 14, 2015.

[16] Fowler, R. (2011 July 13). "Moderation vs. Abstinence: What's More Effective?" The Fix. Accessed May 14, 2015.

[17] Shallow, P. (2014 October 9). "#14 Days: Moderation, a radical option in treating addiction." CBS News. Accessed May 14, 2015.

[18] "Wasting the Best and the Brightest: Substance Abuse at America's Colleges and Universities." (March 2007). CASA Columbia. Accessed May 14, 2015.

[19] Jaffe, A. (2011 March 9). "Abstinence Is Not the Only Option." Psychology Today. Accessed May 14, 2015.

[20] Ibid.

[21] Ibid.

[22] Annual Causes of Death, By Cause 2013

> "To optimize care for those who are
> addicted, it would be ideal to connect
> harm reduction and abstinence
> treatment into a continuum."

Gradualism Is the Key to Recovery from Addiction

Scott H. Kellogg

In the following viewpoint, Scott Kellogg argues that harm-reduction strategies and abstinence-only strategies address the needs of different groups. To bridge the gap between them, he suggests gradualism with the ultimate goal of cessation of drug and alcohol use and mind-body healing. He methodically reviews existing literature and builds his case for establishing a continuum with gradualism as the bridge. He also takes potential counterarguments into account. Kellogg, PhD, is a clinical psychologist and addiction psychologist in private practice in New York City. He is also a Clinical Assistant Professor in New York University's Department of Psychology.

As you read, consider the following questions:

1. What is gradualism, according to this viewpoint?
2. According to this viewpoint, what is the strength of harm reduction?
3. What has to happen for the gradualism concept to work?

Reprinted from "Gradualism and Progressive Addiction Treatment Reform," by Scott H. Kellogg, Elsevier Inc., December 2003. With permission from Elsevier.

The main thrust of this paper is to build a bridge between the abstinence-based and harm reduction treatment communities. This approach, called "gradualism," is centered on trying to create a therapeutic continuum that builds on the strengths of both the harm reduction and abstinence approaches, while trying to reduce their respective shortcomings. Although there has been some work that seeks to integrate harm reduction in abstinence-oriented settings (Denning, 2001; Marlatt, Blume, & Parks, 2001), the focus here is on integrating abstinence into harm-reduction endeavors.

The Categorization of Harm Reduction Activities

Harm reduction is an umbrella term that covers a wide range of interventions. These take place in different settings, have varying goals, and are directed toward diverse populations. As an aid in developing a dialogue between the harm reduction and abstinence worlds, the compendium of harm-reduction approaches have been examined from three perspectives. The first connects the intervention with the diagnostic group that it is best suited for; the second groups interventions by the goal or goals that they are intended to achieve; and the third looks at interventions in terms of the motivational state of the substance-user or patient.

[...]

The interventions that are centered on keeping people alive tend to be aimed at preventing people from dying or seriously damaging themselves due to the direct effects of drug and alcohol use. The time focus of these interventions is frequently very immediate.

The approaches that focus on helping people stay healthy include those that attempt to protect the substance user from HIV, hepatitis B & C, and other negative consequences that can come from the direct use of drugs and alcohol and/or from being in situations in which drugs and alcohol are used (i.e., safety glassware). The time perspective is, generally, somewhat longer than those in the "staying alive" group.

The "getting better" group includes interventions that look more to control and reduce use – if not necessarily eliminate it. As can be seen from the list, most of these interventions have some kind of therapist-patient or physician-patient aspect to them, while the other two groups are more focused on paraphernalia and education.

Some of the concerns about harm reduction interventions can be clarified, if not necessarily resolved, through the use of this goal typology. For example, there has been some distress expressed over the therapeutic value of low threshold methadone programs (Ball & Wijngaart, 1994) in that continued drug use may be a common occurrence (Reuter, 1994). However, low threshold programs have been found to reduce HIV infection because they lead to lower levels of heroin abuse – even if they do not result in the rehabilitation of most of the patients (Rezza, 1994). In this respect, they meet the first two goals, if not the third. Wodak (1994) argues that this is not necessarily without some therapeutic potential as many drug- and alcohol-dependent persons do eventually terminate their use, and that "simply keeping alcohol- and drug-dependent people alive and well for as long as possible is a very important component of treatment" (p. 804).

The third harm reduction categorization seeks to look at the relationship between intervention and motivational state. For the most part, harm-reduction approaches and abstinence-only approaches are fundamentally addressing themselves to the needs of different groups. That is, the ideal target group for reduced-use interventions would be individuals who: (1) would quality for a DSM-IV diagnosis of alcohol or substance abuse or perhaps meet the minimum criteria for a DSM-IV dependence diagnosis; and (2) who are seeking to reduce but not discontinue their involvement with drugs and alcohol (Klaw & Humphreys, 2000; Larimer & Marlatt, 1990; Marlatt, Larimer, Baer, & Quigley, 1993a). One of the positives of this option is that by giving these individuals an opportunity to attempt moderation, a number of them will then chose to cease using drugs or alcohol (Marlatt et al., 1993a; Marlatt, Somers, & Tapert, 1993b; Tatarsky, 1998). In terms of men and women who would qualify for a diagnosis of alcohol or substance dependence, abstinence-oriented programs serve the needs of those who wish to stop using, while harm reduction interventions serve the needs of those who are not in treatment, do not presently wish to be, and may not be ready to discontinue their substance use. Again, some of the abstinence-harm reduction conflicts (Szalavitz, 2000-2001) are unnecessary since all of these approaches are catering to the needs of different audiences.

The harm reduction literature does not seem to be particularly bound by diagnostic categories; however, an informal motivational typology of substance users does emerge from the literature. This consists of: (a) those who are rationally choosing to use substances; (b) those who are unwilling to stop using at the present time (Westermeyer, n.d., a, c); and (c) those who are unable to stop at the present time (Westermeyer, n.d., a, c).

Harm reduction interventions for the first group would primarily be educational (i.e., DanceSafe, n.d.), but could also include substance-use management interventions (Denning & Little, 2001; Marlatt et al., 1993a; Moderation Management, n.d.). The second group includes those who are not ready to change their use pattern because they feel that their alcohol and drug use serves a purpose (Director, 2002; Tatarsky, 1998, This issue). As Tatarsky (1998) noted, "people use substances because they address some psychological, social, or biological needs.... [and] substances may come to serve important psychological functions that help the user cope more effectively" (p. 11). In addition to coping and self-medication functions (Khantzian, 1985; Kohut, 1977), the use of substances may be intimately connected with identities or relationships that appear to be central to the person's sense of self (Biernacki, 1986; Kellogg, 1993; Moore, 1990), and the discontinuation of use may result in the disruption of various social networks. Lastly, the prospect of treatment itself may appear to be unattractive (Denning, 2001; Marlatt et al., 2001; Roche, Evans, & Stanton, 1997; Springer, 2003; Westermeyer, n.d., b).

In terms of intervention, patients in this group could be, and frequently are, understood within a stages of change model (Denning & Little, 2001; Prochaska, DiClemente, & Norcross, 1992;

Springer, 2002), and Motivational Interviewing is a recommended technique (Denning, 2001; Denning & Little, 2001; Miller, Zweben, DiClemente, & Rychtarik, 1995; Springer, 2003; Westermeyer, n.d., a). The purpose of the encounter would be to help them move along the continuum toward taking some kind of action. A psychotherapeutic intervention might be focused on discerning the personal meaning and symbolism of the drug use, evaluating the cost-benefit analysis involved in the decision to keep using (Tatarsky, 1998), understanding the relationship between trauma and substance use (Springer, 2002, 2003), clarifying their drug-related identities and social networks (Biernacki, 1986; Kellogg, 1993), and understanding their conception of their personal life alternatives.

In contrast, the third group consists of those who are "unable" to stop. To see people as being unable to stop leads to what might be called the harm reduction of despair. In one approach, which humanistically emphasizes the needs of these terribly addicted users, harm reduction interventions may serve as a kind psychosocial hospice (see also Gelormino, 2002); a way of "being with" people who are incurably ill, a way of walking with them on a journey toward death. The other approach, which takes more of a societal view, is to see these highly addicted patients as a disease vector, be it for Hepatitis C, HIV, or crime; here, the emphasis becomes one of reducing the harm to the surrounding community. The covert (or not so covert) message, however, may be that they no longer matter as individuals (Ibrahim, 1996).

Harm Reduction as a Pathway to Abstinence

Gradualism, which has a great deal in common with the work of Marlatt (Marlatt, 1996, 1998a, 1998b; Marlatt & Kilmer, 1998; Marlatt et al., 1993 a, b, 2001), seeks to create a continuum between the world of harm reduction interventions and the abstinence-oriented treatment field. Again, this approach differs from other calls for integration (Denning, 2001; Marlatt et al., 2001) because there is a much greater emphasis on making abstinence the eventual endpoint of most harm-reduction enterprises. This paradigm would combine the harm reduction emphases on outreach to the addicted, incremental change, and gradual healing with the abstinence-oriented therapeutic perspective that the use of substances in an addictive or abusive manner is antithetical to the growth and wellbeing of humans. As will be discussed below, this also means using the full compendium of recovery oriented interventions. Instead of being an abstinence-only model, this combined approach could best be understood as an "abstinence-eventually" model.

The strength of the harm reduction approach is in its ability to connect and form relationships (Tatarsky, This issue; Westermeyer, n.d., b). There is certainly something quite striking and quite noble about the outreach workers who go into potentially dangerous and unpleasant situations to make contact with societal "outcasts" (Springer, 2003). There is also something compelling about the creation of centers or subcultures for drug users in which they receive acceptance and welcome (Mechanic, 1996), and where they are greeted with the attitude of, "What can I do to help you?" rather than that of "Here is what you must do" (Westermeyer, n.d., b, p. 1). The warmth of this approach may be a manifestation of what Dean James Parks Morton (1996) referred to as a spirituality of being "radically welcoming," and these interventions could also serve as an entry point to a life-change process.

Some harm reduction advocates might argue that gradualism is not necessary because harm reduction already includes abstinence as part of its continuum of care. This is not the case for two reasons. While some do believe that abstinence is a part of harm reduction (Marlatt et al., 2001), others do not. Roche et al. (1997) have clearly made the case that abstinence-oriented approaches should not be included under the harm-reduction umbrella.

The mixed feelings about the incorporation of abstinence in the model may also reflect some confusion and lack of clarity about the ultimate goal of the harm reduction enterprise. For example, Westermeyer (n.d., a) argued that, "small reductions are better than no reductions …[and] a …small improvement can pave the path for further reductions of drug use…. eventually to the point of abstinence" (p. 1). Tatarsky (1998), while acknowledging the desirability of abstinence as an ideal, maintained that, "the ideal outcome of this approach is to support the user in reducing the harmfulness of substance use to the point where it has minimal negative impact on other areas of his or her life. Whether the outcome is moderation or abstinence depends on what is practically realistic for the client, and emerges from the treatment process (p. 12)." Single (1997), in turn, goes a bit further and writes that, "Harm reduction is simply neutral about the long-term goals of intervention" (p. 8). The Harm Reduction Coalition, in their list of principles, sees the "quality of individual and community life and well-being – not necessarily cessation of all drug use – as the criteria for successful interventions and policies" (Harm Reduction Coalition, n.d., p. 1).

This neutrality about the ultimate goal of treatment also separates harm reduction from gradualism. The problem with neutrality is that it runs the risk of encouraging stagnation, of not fostering a kind of therapeutic or healing momentum.

This opposition to making abstinence the ultimate, if not the immediate, goal may well be connected to some of the social origins of the harm reduction approach, and it may be consistent with what Pearson (1991) called the "Orphan" archetype. In this vision, addicted people are seen as an oppressed and disenfranchised group. Not infrequently, they have been the victims of emotional, physical, and/or sexual abuse (Springer, 2003). The result is a network or community of wounded people who seek to care and nurture each other, while sharing contempt for the forces and symbols of authority. In this light, traditional drug-treatment programs are certainly seen as authoritarian and punitive.

Building the Continuum

Perhaps one way to understand how a gradualist continuum could exist would be to see it in terms of a developmental model involving child and parental images. The high level of acceptance of addicted people found in harm-reduction settings is likely to be experienced

E-Cigarettes and Quitting

Most researchers and public health professionals agree that e-cigarettes and other vaping devices are less harmful than smoked cigarettes, because they do not contain tobacco, the leading contributor to the majority of negative health effects associated with smoking. When used as a complete replacement, rather than in addition to cigarettes, they are a preferable alternative for smokers who haven't had success with medically proven approaches.

But are they really a good option for smokers who want to cut down or quit smoking? Not necessarily. While a few studies have found that e-cigarettes can help reduce smoking, most show that e-cigarette use does not significantly reduce cigarette use, and several found that people who use e-cigarettes may be less likely to successfully quit smoking.

Overall, the limited research findings are inconclusive. A recent scientific review concluded that the data available on the role of e-cigarettes in smoking cessation are limited due to a small number of studies and a lack of quality data. Many studies are currently underway to help determine whether using e-cigarettes to quit or reduce smoking is a good choice.

"Can E-Cigarettes Help You Quit Smoking?" The National Center on Addiction and Substance Abuse, December 2016.

as a form of unconditional positive regard, of caring without demands. It is well reflected in the harm reduction emphasis on meeting the patient "where they're at" (Denning, 2001; Denning & Little, 2001, p. 1; Harm Reduction Coalition, n.d.). This open nurturing may do a great deal to help build relationships and get these addicted persons re-connected again. The harm reduction site becomes something of a "holding environment" (Greenberg & Mitchell, 1983; Winnicott, 1963/1965). This may well work because, in my opinion, there is, among many of these patients, a deep longing for good, nurturing, affirming authority – perhaps especially for good fathers (Bly, 1992; Thompson, 1991). However, the good parent does not simply love unconditionally. And while it may be important to meet the patient where he or she is, it may not be such a good idea to leave him or her there (see also Gelormino, 2002). As Goethe wrote, and Viktor Frankl (1985) affirmed, "If I accept you as you are, I will make you worse; However, if I treat you as though you are what you are capable of becoming, I help you become that" (quoted in Mayo, 1996, p. 240). The good parent not only nurtures, but also affirms the possibility within the child. Within the context of the harm reduction classification schemes, this means working to keep them alive, to protect their health, and to help them to heal and get better. The parent that does not take action to help a child who is pain or in danger, may not be felt to be a good parent, and, since the patients themselves, for the most part, do not think that the use of drugs is a good or life-affirming activity, there is a question as to what kind of message the psychotherapist is giving if he or she does not ultimately (even if not immediately) direct them toward abstinence.

From this perspective, the eventual emphasis on abstinence, within a context of seeing both the woundedness and the potential within these individuals, also becomes a form of nurturing. The next step, then, would be for people to make a successful transition to an empowering, recovery-oriented treatment, and, hopefully, to a healthy, productive, and drug-free life. The comprehensive needle exchange program described by Majoor and Rivera (This issue) appears to embody many of these dynamics.

Tatarsky (1998) has made the point that some patients can learn to moderate and control their use of drugs and alcohol. Marlatt et al. (1993a), in their review of the literature, found that controlled drinking was a not uncommon treatment outcome. Taking this as a possibility, abstinence would still have a role here. Moderation Management, the self-help group dedicated to helping people control their alcohol use, asks members to refrain from drinking for 30 days before beginning a moderation program. They also ask them to spend that time analyzing their patterns of use and the meaning and role that alcohol has for them (Moderation Management, n.d.). Marlatt (Marlatt & Gordon, 1985) also saw abstinence as a preliminary step for those who might be able to moderate their use.

However, for the gradualist continuum to work, not only would the harm reduction field have to modify its perspective, but also the treatment community would need to transform itself as well. A good place to start would be to bring some of this "welcoming spirituality" to their treatment facilities, to create and foster an atmosphere that is less harsh and less judgmental (Denning, 2001; Marlatt et al., 2001; Roche et al., 1997; Springer, 2003). This means building on a crucial insight of the harm reduction movement – that healing and recovery are more likely to come through the development of relationship (Denning, 2001; Tatarsky, This issue), rather than through the imposition of authority. The next step would be to realize that we are living in a time of increasing therapeutic creativity in which there are more and more therapies that are helpful for addicted or drug-using people. One metaphor that could illuminate this is the idea of the "treatment mosaic," an idea that is essentially synonymous with what is known as the treatment menu concept (Miller et al., 1995). A treatment mosaic would provide patients with a full range of therapeutic possibilities, and they would be encouraged to utilize the ones that resonated with them.

In another version of this argument, Marlatt and Kilmer (1998), building on the work of Bickel, have made the case that treatment has the potential to be an "alternative reinforcer" (p. 570) that could replace drug and alcohol use. For this to happen, treatment must be made attractive and patients must be treated well. As part of the process of making treatment a positive experience, patients, again, should be given a range of recovery options.

With this in mind, an abstinence-oriented healing network would want to utilize the entire range of existing therapeutic approaches that have been shown to have some utility. These would include the full range of self-help and support groups including Alcoholics Anonymous, Narcotics Anonymous, other Twelve-Step fellowships, SMART Recovery®, Rational Recovery®, Women (and Men) for Sobriety, and S.O.S. (see also Velten's comments in

Marlatt, 1998a, p. 21). In terms of psychological interventions for patients, there is relapse prevention (Marlatt & Gordon, 1985), other cognitive-behavioral interventions (Wright, Beck, Newman, & Liese, 1993), psychodynamically-based, addiction-oriented, long-term psychotherapy (Director, 2002), and the contingency-management and voucher-incentive behavioral programs (Higgins, Alessi, & Dantona, 2002; Petry, Martin, Cooney, & Kranzler, 2000; Stitzer, Iguchi, Kidorf, & Bigelow, 1993). Over the past few years, there have been a number of interesting and creative developments in the therapeutic community field and, ideally, these would continue. Clearly, the further development of therapeutic communities that incorporate patients who are being treated with methadone and other maintenance medications would also be a major breakthrough (De Leon, 1997).

There is also a growing literature on the "natural recovery" experience that addresses how people recover from addiction problems without self-help or program attendance (Biernacki, 1986; Granville & Cloud, 1996; Stall & Biernacki, 1986), and the insights from these studies could be incorporated into treatment. For those who are interested, religiously based treatment programs may be a possibility (Muffler, Langrod, Richardson, & Ruiz, 1997). Alternative medicine and holistic health practices may be helpful adjunctively as well (Nebelkopf, 1981), and these could include acupuncture (Moner, 1996), herbal teas and medicines (Odierna, n.d.), and yoga (Shaffer, LaSalvia, & Stein, 1997). Ibogaine may also be helpful for some as well (Alper, Lotsof, Frenken, Daniel, & Bastiaans, 1999). Lastly, there are an increasing number of medications available to help support efforts at recovery including methadone (in adequate doses; D'Aunno & Pollack, 2002; D'Aunno & Vaughn, 1992), LAAM, buprenorphine/naloxone, naltrexone, disulfiram, and acamprosate.

The Issue of Relapse

The final argument in favor of the gradualist continuum is the high rate of relapse among alcohol- and drug-dependent patients.

Even abstinence advocates like Owen (in Owen & Marlatt, 2001), believe that only half of the patients in alcohol treatment will be likely to achieve sobriety. O'Brien and McLellan (1996), in a paper that strongly defended the efficacy of substance abuse treatment, put the treatment success rate for alcohol dependence at approximately 50%, for opioid dependence using methadone at 60%, and for cocaine dependence using a contingency management protocol, at 55%. (It should be noted that contingency management, while effective, is not a commonly used treatment intervention.) They repeatedly stress that relapse is a commonly occurring phenomenon, and that the treatment for substance and alcohol dependence should be considered a long-term endeavor.

The gradualist model being presented here may be able to respond to this situation. First, by offering a much wider range of options in a positive and affirming way and allowing patients to choose among them, the treatment field may be able to improve on its record of success. Second, by creating a continuum of care, a therapeutic "safety net" can be created (see also Marlatt, 1998b). The goal would be that the life and health of relapsing patients would be preserved through the work of the harm-reduction organizations, and, using the momentum of a gradualist approach, they would be able to return more rapidly to a drug- and alcohol-free life.

Conclusion

We are currently living in a time of rich therapeutic possibilities for working substance-using and substance-dependent patients. This creativity is taking place both within the harm-reduction and abstinence-oriented spheres. To optimize care for those who are addicted, it would be ideal to connect harm reduction and abstinence treatment into a continuum that has the cessation of drug and alcohol use and the healing of mind and body as the desired end point. Gradualism has been put forward as an organizing principle to facilitate this development.

Periodical and Internet Sources Bibliography

The following articles have been selected to supplement the diverse views presented in this chapter.

Corliss Bayles, "Using Mindfulness in a Harm Reduction Approach to Substance Abuse Treatment: A Literature Review," International Journal of Behavioral Consultation and Therapy, 2014, http://psycnet.apa.org/fulltext/2014-38134-007.pdf.

Morgan Coe, "The Adoption of Harm Reduction by Abstinence Program Staff: A Qualitative Analysis," University of Massachusetts Amherst ScholarWorks, 2016, https://scholarworks.umass.edu/cgi/viewcontent.cgi?referer=https://www.google.com/&httpsredir=1&article=1400&context=masters_theses_2.

HAMS Harm Reduction Network, "Harm Elimination Contrasted with Harm Reduction," HAMS Harm Reduction Network, 2008, http://hams.cc/elimination/.

Neil McKeganey, "From Harm Reduction to Drug User Abstinence: A Journey in Drug Treatment Policy," Journal of Substance Abuse, 2011, https://www.tandfonline.com/doi/full/10.3109/14659891.2011.580228.

Michael Musalek, "Reduction of Harmful Consumption versus Total Abstinence in Addiction Treatment," Neuropsychiatry, 2013, http://www.jneuropsychiatry.org/peer-review/reduction-of-harmful-consumption-versus-total-abstinence-in-addiction-treatment-neuropsychiatry.pdf.

The Recovery Village, "What Is the Harm Reduction Approach to Substance Abuse Treatment?," The Recovery Village, June 23, 2017, https://www.therecoveryvillage.com/recovery-blog/harm-reduction-approach-substance-abuse-treatment/#gref.

Vantage Point, "The Harm Reduction Model versus Abstinence in Recovery," Vantage Point, 2018, https://vantagepointrecovery.com/the-harm-reduction-model-versus-abstinence-in-recovery/.

CHAPTER 4

Does Law Enforcement Help or Hinder Harm Reduction?

Chapter Preface

L aw enforcement officials are the ones responsible for the front-line interaction with those accused of drug use, possession, manufacturing, sale, and purchase. Law enforcement must translate legal code into action on the street. Many are forced into the role of psychologist or social worker without having the necessary training for such roles. There is a predisposition toward arrest and incarceration that makes access to treatment less likely. The Law Enforcement and HIV Network provides an example in which mutual cooperation between the police and public health agencies successfully work to help the drug user. One way to encourage police participation is to understand their priorities to serve and protect and communicate harm reduction in a manner consistent with those priorities. Some factors must also be considered, including the use of local, state, and federal law. However, these laws must take into account not only the individual's liberty and body integrity, that is, to make decisions about one's own body, but also the public health safety of entire communities. These are tough, ethical decisions that public health authorities and law-making agencies must address. Still, harm reduction is viewed as a means to protect human rights.

Within the United States, presidential administration stances on the war against drugs translates to the federal budget, which upon analysis, favors abstinence and incarceration vs. progressive harm reduction.

On a more international scale, the United Nations issued a Political Statement in 2016 to end the AIDS epidemic by 2030. This statement included the need to fast-track AIDS response within five years. Police engagement is necessary to achieve both the short- and long-term goals.

In the following chapter, authors ranging from former police officers to the Library of Congress examine legal strategies and tactics at all levels and whether they help or hinder harm reduction.

> "Law enforcement can undermine
> the positive effects of existing public
> health interventions that deliver vital
> services to people engaged in drug
> use or sex work and promote the
> health of communities overall."

Mutual Trust Between Law Enforcement and Community Health Systems Is Needed

David Cloud

In the following viewpoint, excerpted for length, David Cloud argues that fear of criminalization can drive drug users further underground, making access to treatment and other health services less likely. Law enforcement does not have the necessary training to deal with people with need for treatment. Law enforcement and community health systems must establish mutual trust. David Cloud, JD, MPH, is a senior program associate for the Vera Institute of Justice's Substance Use and Mental Health Program. He examines mass incarceration and public health systems as they pertain to the community and justice reform.

"First Do No Harm: Advancing Public Health in Policing Practices," by David Cloud, Vera Institute of Justice, November 2015. Reprinted by permission.

As you read, consider the following questions:

1. Which minor offenses become grounds for arrest?
2. How many Americans believe the federal government should give heroin and cocaine users access to treatment rather than prosecute them?
3. Which groups does the war on drugs target?

Millions of medically vulnerable and socially marginalized people cycle through the criminal justice system each year because of serious structural problems entrenched in American society. The absence of a coherent and effective social safety net means that individuals lack access to health care, mental health care, social services, and housing options in their communities. In cities and communities across the nation, police act as reluctant social workers without the benefit of training and treatment providers of last resort for people with chronic, unmet health and social service needs. They must assume these roles because of laws and policies that have criminalized quality-of-life offenses and minor drug-related behaviors, with the greatest burden falling upon the poor and communities of color.

Unfortunately, the cultural divide and lack of cooperation among law enforcement, public health agencies, and harm reduction advocates amplify and sustain these problems.

As a former police chief and currently a chief deputy sheriff with more than 32 years' experience in law enforcement and the former executive director of one of New York City's first syringe-exchange programs and current executive director of the Harm Reduction Coalition for more than 20 years, we recognize the need for joint leadership, a shared vision, and mutual trust among police and community health systems. It is imperative for improving how local governments address vexing health and social problems such as drug use, mental illness, sex work, and poverty. We must work together in strengthening our partnerships so that we may improve and sustain the health and safety of our communities.

Introduction

Many of the issues that both public health and law enforcement agencies address in the communities they serve are rooted in health inequities, violence, trauma, racism, and poverty. As a result of the shortcomings of underresourced public health and social service systems and a longstanding lack of cooperation between law enforcement and community health agencies, millions of medically vulnerable and socially marginalized people are caught up in the criminal justice system each year. Minor offenses—such as drug possession, prostitution, public intoxication, loitering, and trespassing—frequently become grounds for arrest, incarceration, and criminal records.

The failed promises of the deinstitutionalization movement—in which the primary locus of psychiatric treatment shifted from long-term care in state hospitals to community-based settings without adequate public funding—have led to a chronic shortage of outpatient mental health services, income assistance, and housing and employment support that many people with chronic psychiatric disabilities need to live successfully in their communities.[1] As a result—and against the backdrop of the largest expansion of the criminal justice system in U.S. history—police officers have found themselves routinely serving as de-facto street-corner psychiatrists and frontline mental health workers whenever a family cannot manage a loved one who is suffering an acute episode of mental illness or a person with untreated psychiatric needs behaves erratically or menacingly in public.[2] Police also frequently encounter people who are homeless or marginally housed during patrol and may be involved in what are commonly called quality-of-life crimes—e.g., loitering, panhandling, and public intoxication. For instance, in Los Angeles County in 2013, homeless people accounted for 14 percent of all arrests, and the police spent more than three-quarters of the $100 million that the county allocated to combat homelessness that year.[3]

Concurrently, punitive sentencing laws, such as mandatory minimums, and policing practices, such as sting operations and drug sweeps, that arose under the auspices of the drug war have proven ineffective in reducing the prevalence of drug use or curbing the sale or manufacture of illegal drugs.[4] Instead, these tactics have generated large numbers of arrests and incarcerations for mostly minor drug-related crimes, backlogging courts, overcrowding correctional facilities, and taxing public resources. A 2005 survey, conducted by the National Association of Chiefs of Police showed that 82 percent of police chiefs and sheriffs said that the national war on drugs has been unsuccessful in reducing drug use.[5] A 2014 poll found that two-thirds of Americans believe that government should focus on providing people who use heroin and cocaine with access to treatment rather than prosecuting them.[6] In 2013, police in the United States made more than 11.3 million arrests, of which the greatest number were for drug-related crimes. Of all these arrests, 83 percent were for possession of a controlled substance.[7] Moreover, aggressive drug war policing tactics are waged disproportionately against racial and ethnic minorities residing in urban environments. Black and Latino people residing in urban, low income neighborhoods are far more likely to be stopped, searched, arrested, and jailed for drug offenses than white people, despite comparable prevalence of drug use and sales.[8]

These enforcement practices detrimentally affect important social determinants of health by obstructing social and economic mobility among residents of disadvantaged communities, as arrest and criminal records can hamper educational and employment prospects for a lifetime.[9] Moreover, the fear of arrest and exposure to incarceration can promote poor health practices that lead to the spread of infectious disease within a community and the increased risk of fatal overdose among people who inject drugs.

Through the adoption of harm reduction and health promotion practices—and in light of reforms in both the criminal justice system and national health care—community health providers and law enforcement agencies have new opportunities to work together to promote access to health services for marginalized populations and ameliorate the harms associated with needless cycles of arrest and incarceration.

In contrast to abstinence-based interventions, harm reduction is a set of practical strategies that aims to minimize the negative impacts of drug use and other high-risk behaviors, even when people are not ready or able to give up these behaviors. Harm reduction principles were initially developed to reduce the spread of HIV, particularly in communities with many injection drug users. Health promotion, as defined by the World Health Organization (WHO), is "the process of enabling people to increase control over, and to improve, their health." Successful health promotion initiatives aim to empower individuals in accessing healthcare, improve community capacity and collective efficacy, and act as social and environmental interventions."[10]

This report focuses on how police can integrate harm reduction and health promotion into their work, and the ways in which police and community health providers can partner to strengthen and expand diversion programs, keeping people who are more in need of health and social services than punishment out of the justice system. While policing practices have a large impact on the health of communities in general, they disparately affect particularly marginalized groups, including people engaged in sex work or injection drug use, homeless individuals, and people with chronic psychiatric disabilities. This report describes interagency strategies to reduce unnecessary arrests and incarceration and promote the health of people within these groups.

Background

Because of deficiencies in community mental health systems, police are routinely called to respond to situations where a person is experiencing a psychiatric crisis.[11] Studies estimate that seven to 10 percent of all police interactions involve people with a mental illness, and officers working in larger police departments report an average of six monthly encounters involving a person in a state of psychiatric distress.[12] Police themselves are emotionally affected by these growing interactions and often report inadequate training, deficient resources, frustration in accessing services, and conflicted feelings about their role as de-facto mental health workers.[13]

Without the resources police officers need, such as specialized training and alternative diversion options, these mental health emergencies can quickly escalate into violence and result in serious physical injury or death to individuals involved, including bystanders or police officers themselves. Though police agencies are not required to collect data or report on injuries or fatalities occurring during psychiatric emergencies, the Maine Attorney General's Office reported that, from 2000 to 2012, 42 percent of people shot by police had a mental health diagnosis.[14] Anecdotal reports from across the country suggest an equivalent national gure.[15] According to an analysis by the *Washington Post*, 124 people with mental illness have been shot and killed by police in the United States during the first six months of 2015.[16] Many of these tragedies have prompted civil lawsuits and federal investigations into the hiring practices, training, and culture of local police departments.[17]

In non-emergency situations, police officers report being more likely to arrest someone who displays signs of mental illness for petty offenses if they believe that jail is the only option to provide the person with access to food, a place to sleep, and basic health services. This is known as "mercy booking" and, despite good intentions, it is a driver of unnecessary jail incarceration among medically vulnerable communities.[18] Police also regularly transport people displaying signs of psychosis or disorientation to emergency rooms, even if they may not require urgent intervention and would be better served by an outpatient consultation. These tactics are symptomatic of the lack of options or training available to police officers.[19]

Moreover, law enforcement can undermine the positive effects of existing public health interventions that deliver vital services to people engaged in drug use or sex work and promote the health of communities overall. For example, in several U.S. cities, law enforcement and prosecutors use a person's possession of condoms as evidence to file prostitution charges. This practice makes many sex workers reluctant to carry condoms, thus increasing their risk of HIV and other sexually transmitted infections as well as unwanted pregnancies.[20] Drug laws and policies direct police officers to search and arrest people suspected of possessing or using small amounts of drugs and paraphernalia or partaking in minor drug transactions. While such measures are often meant to reduce and eliminate these behaviors, research has shown that the fear of criminalization serves only to drive many people engaged in drug use or sex work further underground, decreasing their access to treatment and health care services, and increasing their risk of acquiring or transmitting infectious diseases in their social networks and communities.[21]

Injection drug users (IDUs) are one of the groups at greatest risk of contracting HIV, Hepatitis B and C, and other communicable diseases.[22] The Centers for Disease Control (CDC) estimate that about one-third of AIDS-related deaths can be attributed to injection drug use. Recent surveys indicate that about one-third of active, young IDUs (ages 18 to 30) and approximately 70 to 90 percent of older and former IDUs have the Hepatitis C virus (HCV).[23] Harm reduction services, such as syringe exchange programs (SEPs, also known as needle exchange programs), are highly effective in educating people about available treatment and behaviors that prevent infectious disease, providing access and referrals to services, and reducing other negative consequences associated with chronic drug use.[24] SEPs also connect people to drug counseling, evidence-based addiction treatment—including opiate substitution treatments (OST) such as methadone and buprenorphine—and other social services that effectively treat addiction and link individuals to employment and housing assistance.

The fear of arrest among drug users also increases the risk of overdose—the leading cause of injury-related death in the United States.[25] A recent study using New York City mortality data from 1990 to 1999 found accidental drug overdose was significantly higher in police precincts with higher misdemeanor arrest rates.

The study's authors suggest that, because most overdoses are witnessed by other drug users, the fear of arrest and prosecution often makes them delay or refrain from calling 911 for emergency intervention. Fear also incentivizes people to use drugs in more secluded, less visible settings that may not be witnessed at all or harder for emergency services to access. Without a timely response from emergency medical services, otherwise preventable deaths will occur.[26]

A large body of medical and social science research demonstrates that OST programs successfully reduce heroin use, fatal overdoses, HIV transmission, criminal activity, and financial burdens among drug users.[27] However, SEPs and OST programs are often located in neighborhoods with a high police presence and often become targets for investigations and arrests despite their legality. Because many police agencies have misconceptions about how harm reduction programs operate and what value these programs have in promoting public safety, police officers may be directed to confiscate syringes or arrest program participants, directly interfering with the benefits these programs provide to community health.[28] Moreover, non-white users of SEPs are more likely to be stopped by police in a program's vicinity and more likely to stop using such programs as a result.[29] Thus, the effectiveness of and equal access to harm reduction programs is significantly dependent upon police cooperation.[30]

[…]

Notes

1. Gerald N. Grob, From Asylum to Community (Princeton, NJ: Princeton University Press, 1991); and Richard G. Frank and Sherry A. Glied, Better But Not Well: Mental Health Policy in the United States since 1950 (Baltimore, MD: Johns Hopkins University Press, 2006).

2. Soung Lee, Scott Brunero, Greg Fairbrother, and Darrin Cowan, "Pro ling police presentations of mental health consumers to an emergency department," International Journal of Mental Health Nursing 17, no. 5 (2008): 311-316; and Oren M. Gur, "Persons with Mental Illness in the Criminal Justice System: Police Interventions to Prevent Violence and Criminalization," Journal of Police Crisis Negotiations 10, no. 1-2 (2010): 220-240; and Linda A. Teplin and Nancy S. Pruett, "Police as streetcorner psychiatrist: Managing the mentally ill," International Journal of Law and Psychiatry 15, no. 2 (1992): 139-156.

3. Charles Davis, "Under the Bridge: The Crime of Living Without a Home in Los Angeles," The Intercept, July 25, 2015, perma.cc/ C8K6-69KY.

4. L.D. Johnson, P. M. O'Malley, R. A. Miech, J. G. Bachman, and J.E. Schulenberg, Monitoring the Future National Survey Results on Drug Use: 1975-2013: Overview. Key Findings on Adolescent Drug Use (Ann Arbor, MI: Institute for Social Research, University of Michigan, 2014).

5. National Association of Chiefs of Police, 18th Annual National Survey Results of Police Chiefs & Sheriffs (Titusville, FL: NACOP, 2005), perma.cc/H4Y2-HRDW.

6. Pew Research Center, "America's New Drug Policy Landscape: Two- Thirds Favor Treatment, Not Jail, for Use of Heroin, Cocaine," April 2, 2014, perma.cc/6EAT-74JF.

7. Federal Bureau of Investigation, "Crime in the United States 2013 - Arrests," perma.cc/ AU5C-U4CX.

8. Jamie Fellner, "Race, Drugs, and Law Enforcement in the United States," Stanford Law and Policy Review 20, no. 2 (2009): 257-292; Center for Constitutional Rights, 2011 NYPD Stop and Frisk Statistics (New York: CCR, 2011), perma.cc/2Z7K-BECM; National Association for the Advancement of Colored People (NAACP), Criminal Justice Fact Sheet, (Baltimore, MD: NAACP, 2015), perma. cc/D6N8-6ZFF; and The Brookings Institution Social Mobility Memos, "How the War on Drugs Damages Black Social Mobility," Sept. 30, 2014, perma.cc/3R2A-63UD.

9. G. J. Chin, "Race, the War on Drugs, and the Collateral Consequences of Criminal Conviction," Journal of Gender, Race & Justice 6 (2002): 253-277; Social determinants of health (SDH)— as defined by the World Health Organization—refers to the circumstances in which people are born, grow up, live, work, and age, as well as systems designed to deal with illness. According to this widely accepted model, health is influenced by a range of social, economic, and political forces beyond the control of the individual. See Michael Marmot, "Social Determinants of Health Inequalities," The Lancet 365, no. 9464 (2005): 1099-1104.

10. World Health Organization, "Health Promotion," perma.cc/Z9E6- SWW3.

11. H. J. Steadman, F. C. Osher, Pamela Clark Robbins, B. Case, and S. Samuels, "Prevalence of serious mental illness among jail inmates," Psychiatric Services 60, no. 6 (2009): 761-765; and National Institute of Mental Health, "Serious Mental Illness (SMI) Among U.S. Adults," perma.cc/M47T-2PHR; and Teplin and Pruett, 1992, 139-156.

12. Randy Borum, "Police perspectives on responding to mentally ill people in crisis: Perceptions of program effectiveness," Mental Health Law & Policy Faculty Publications (1998); and Martha Williams Deane, Henry J. Steadman, Randy Borum, Bonita M. Veysey, and Joseph P. Morrissey, "Emerging partnerships between mental health and law enforcement," Psychiatric Services 50, no. 1(1999): 99-101.

13. Nicola McLean and Lisa A. Marshall, "A front line police perspective of mental health issues and services," Criminal Behavior and Mental Health 20, no.1 (2010): 62-71.

14. Kelley Bouchard, "Across nation, unsettling acceptance when mentally ill in crisis are killed," Portland Press Herald, December 9, 2012, perma.cc/Q7ML-H62T.

15. E. Fuller Torrey, Sheriff Aaron D. Kennard, Donald F. Eslinger, Michael C. Biasotti, and Doris A. Fuller, Justifiable Homicides by Law Enforcement Of cers: What is the Role of Mental Illness? (Arlington, VA: TAC, 2013), perma.cc/U39A-442R.

16 The Washington Post, "Deadly Shootings by Police by Month, 2015," in Distraught People, Deadly Results, perma.cc/J8RV-7T9S.

17. For example, see the settlement agreement in U.S. Department of Justice v. City of Albuquerque (Nov. 10, 2014), perma.cc/Y8W6- 2HeM.

18. Amy Watson and Daniel Luchins, "Paths to jail among mentally ill persons: Service needs and service characteristics," Psychiatric Annals 31, no. 7 (2001); Richard Lamb, Roger Schock, Peter W. Chen, and Bruce Gross, "Psychiatric needs in local jails: emergency issues," The American Journal of Psychiatry 141, no. 6 (1984): 774-777; Linda A. Teplin, "Criminalizing mental disorder: the comparative arrest rate of the mentally ill," American Psychologist 39, no. 7 (1984): 794-803; and Anne Rogers, "Policing Mental Disorder: Controversies, Myths and Realities," Social Policy & Administration 24, no. 3 (1990): 226-236.

19. Richard Lamb,Linda Weinberger, andWalter DeCuir Jr.,"The Police and Mental Health," Psychiatric Services 53, no. 10 (2002): 1266-1271; Teplin and Pruett, 1992, 139-156; Soung Lee et al., 2008, 311-316; Oren M. Gur, "Persons with Mental Illness in the Criminal Justice System: Police Interventions to Prevent Violence and Criminalization," Journal of Police Crisis Negotiations 10, no. 1-2 (2010): 220-240.

20. Human Rights Watch, Sex Workers at Risk: Condoms as Evidence of Prostitution in Four U.S. Cities, (New York, NY: HRW, 2012), perma. cc/S4QG-MX7F.

21. Stephen Koester, "Copping, Running, and Paraphernalia Laws: Contextual Variables and Needle Risk Behavior Among Injection Drug Users in Denver," Human Organization 53, no. 3 (1994): 287-295; Evan Wood, Patricia M. Spittal, Will Small, Thomas Kerr, Kathy Li, Robert S. Hogg, Mark W. Tyndall, Julio SG Montaner, and Martin T. Schechter, "Displacement of Canada's largest public illicit drug market in response to a police crackdown," Canadian Medical Association Journal 170, no. 10 (2004): 1551-1556; and Scott Burris, Kim M. Blankenship, Martin Donoghoe, Susan Sherman, Jon S. Vernick, Patricia Case, Zita Lazzarini, and Stephen Koester, "Addressing the 'Risk Environment' for Injection Drug Users: The Mysterious Case of the Missing Cop," Milbank Quarterly 82, no. 1 (2004): 125-156.

22. Shruti Mehta et al., "Changes in Blood-borne Infection Risk Among Injection Drug Users," Journal of Infectious Diseases 203, no. 5 (2011): 587-594.

23. MiriamJ.Alter,"PreventionofspreadofhepatitisC,"Hepatology36, no. 5B (2002): s93-s98; Centers for Disease Control and Prevention, "HIV and Injection Drug Use in the United States," perma.cc/VMX7- 2gcb; and Centers for Disease Control and Prevention, "Hepatitis C FAQs for Health Professionals," perma.cc/5KHU-HXRZ.

24. Centers for Disease Control and Prevention, "Syringe exchange programs—United States, 2008," Morbidity and Mortality Weekly Report 59, no. 45 (2010): 1488-1491; Alex Wodak and Annie Cooney, Effectiveness of Sterile Needle and Syringe Programming in Reducing HIV/AIDS Among Injecting Drug Users (Geneva: World Health Organization, 2004); I. G. Takacs and Z. Demetrovics, "[The ef cacy of needle exchange programs in the prevention of HIV and hepatitis infection among injecting drug users]," Psychiatria Hungarica: A Magyar Pszichiatriai Tarsasag tudomanyos folyoirata 24, no. 4 (2008): 264-281; and Gay Men's Health Crisis, Syringe Exchange: An Effective Tool in the Fight Against HIV and Drug Abuse (New York, NY: GMHC, 2009).

25. Leo Beletsky, Daliah Heller, Samuel M. Jenness, Alan Neaigus, Camila Gelpi-Acosta, and Holly Hagan, "Syringe access, syringe sharing, and police encounters among people who inject drugs in New York City: a community-level perspective," International Journal of Drug Policy 25, no. 1 (2014): 105-111; Hannah LF Cooper, Don C. Des Jarlais, Barbara Tempalski, Brian H. Bossak, Zev Ross, and Samuel R.

Friedman, "Drug-related arrest rates and spatial access to syringe exchange programs in New York City health districts: Combined effects on the risk of injection-related infections among injectors," Health & Place 18, no. 2 (2012): 218-228; and Evan Wood, Thomas Kerr, Will Small, Jim Jones, Martin T. Schechter, and Mark W. Tyndall, "The impact of a police presence on access to needle exchange programs," Journal of Acquired Immune De ciency Syndromes 34, no. 1 (2003): 116-117.

26. Amy SB Bohnert, Arijit Nandi, Melissa Tracy, Magdalena Cerdá, Kenneth J. Tardiff, David Vlahov, and Sandro Galea, "Policing and risk of overdose mortality in urban neighborhoods," Drug and Alcohol Dependence 113, no. 1 (2011): 62-68.

27. P. Lawrinson et al., "Key Findings from the WHO collaborative study on substitution therapy for opioid dependence and HIV/AID," Addiction 103, no. 9 (2008), 1484-1492.

28. Leo Beletsky, Grace E. Macalino, and Scott Burris, "Attitudes of police of cers toward syringe access, occupational needle-sticks, and drug use: A qualitative study of one city police department in the United States," International Journal of Drug Policy 16, (2005): 267-274; and Leo Beletsky, Jess Cochrane, Anne Sawyer, Chris Serio-Chapman, Marina Smelyanskaya, Jennifer Han, Natanya Rabinowitz, and Susan G. Sherman, "Police encounters among needle exchange clients in Baltimore: drug law enforcement as a structural determinant of health," American Journal of Public Health 105, no. 9 (2015): 1872-1879.

29. Corey Davis, Scott Burris, Julie Kraut-Becher, Kevin Lynch, and David Metzger, "Effects of an intensive street level police intervention on syringe exchange program use in Philadelphia, PA," American Journal of Public Health 95, no. 2 (2005): 233-236.

30. Harm Reduction International, "Needle Exchanges," perma.cc/ UC7X-MY8K.

> *"LEAHN provides a crucial infrastructure that connects police to the HIV sector and communicates harm reduction best practice within the domain of law enforcement."*

Police Culture Benefits from a Special Network to Respond Effectively to HIV

Nick Crofts and Melissa Jardine

In the following viewpoint, Nick Crofts and Melissa Jardine argue law enforcement is responsible for interpreting the "law of the book" to the "law on the street." Yet, they are unprepared. The Law Enforcement and HIV Network (LEAHN) was established to bridge the gap between police and public health. Nick Crofts is a professor at the University of Melbourne and Director, Centre for Law Enforcement & Public Health in Australia. Former police officer Melissa Jardine is Director, Global Law Enforcement & Public Health Association and Gender Advisor & Communications Manager for the Centre for Law Enforcement & Public Health.

"The Role of the Police in the HIV Response: the Law Enforcement and HIV Network," by Nick Crofts and Melissa Jardine, Australian Federation of AIDS Organisations (AFAO), March 2016. Reprinted from Volume 14, No. 1 of HIV Australia, published by the Australian Federation of AIDS Organisations.

As you read, consider the following questions:

1. What is the purpose of LEAHN?
2. How many police officers worldwide have signed the LEAHN Statement of Support?
3. According to this viewpoint, what three misconceptions do civil and non-governmental agencies have about working with police?

P olice are the first responders to a range of complex situations involving criminal, civil or public health related issues, some of which may relate to HIV. Law enforcement, HIV and public health are therefore inextricably linked; however many law enforcement agencies do not perceive these connections.

The Global Commission on HIV and the Law 2012 report clearly outlines the need for reform of policing practice, and the opportunity to recruit police as partners, facilitators and even leaders in HIV prevention strategies.

One significant recommendation in the report[1] is that reform of policy and law must go hand in hand with reform of law enforcement practices and implementation of policy and law by police; critically, these are different activities requiring different focuses.

The report also states: 'In many countries, the law (either on the books or on the streets) dehumanises many of those at highest risk for HIV'[2]

Police are the key group translating 'law on the books' to 'law on the street' (or often acting without reference to the law at all). Police routinely enforce the criminalisation of activities such as drug use or sex work, meaning that law enforcement practices are one of the major determinants of the risk environment for people at greatest risk of HIV.

In many situations police may use existing law to meet more pressing community or political pressures. It is therefore essential that police are engaged as partners in the HIV response and supported to change their approach.

The Law Enforcement and HIV Network (LEAHN) was established to ensure that law enforcement officers and agencies are equipped to support a human rights based response to HIV in their jurisdictions. Set up by police, LEAHN is an international network of people involved in HIV prevention, particularly those working in law enforcement and public health.

LEAHN facilitates knowledge sharing, advocacy and peer education enabling police and public health professionals to share advice and experiences about HIV prevention and harm reduction programs.

Achieving Cultural Change

One of the biggest remaining challenges, as LEAHN sees it, is the need to reform police culture.

Policing 'culture' is subject to a variety of influences that are difficult for an outsider to discern. In many countries, this culture is male-oriented and male-dominated, self-protecting, and embodies the prejudices and attitudes of the wider society.

Changing behaviours is secondary to changing the culture; culture, through peer influence, is often a far stronger determinant of behaviour than police training.

Implementing training within police academies on human rights, harm reduction policing, and the necessity for a partnership approach to addressing HIV – all this is good and necessary, but is not in itself sufficient to change police behaviours.

The closed culture which a new police officer enters after leaving the academy determines many aspects of his or her behavior on the job; and if this is not a culture supportive of human rights and partnerships in the HIV response, the training will be quickly forgotten. Similarly, short-term or one-off training workshops have little impact if the participants return to an unchanged culture and work environment.

To engage police in the response to HIV, it is necessary to understand the world from their point of view, to appreciate the multiple pressures on them, and to ask 'what's in it for them?' Too often, advocacy to police from the HIV sector sounds to them like 'help us do our job'; the usual police response is 'we're too busy doing our job' (as they perceive it to be).

Police agencies worldwide are undergoing budgetary cutbacks; everywhere, they are subject to the same mantra: 'focus on the traditional role of policing, that of identifying and catching criminals; ignore the marginal activities such as partnering with public health'.

What this imperative forgets is that police have always had a critical partnership role in public health – in road trauma, violence and other crime prevention, dealing with mental health crises and many other issues; this role is not marginal, it is central to the police mandate.

The fact that this role is under-recognised and under-rewarded means that police do not immediately understand that their partnership role in HIV prevention and care is part of a normal and central contribution police make to a healthy and safe society.

In many countries, there are structural drivers of counter-productive police behaviours, such as low pay and status and inadequate training.

The global move towards professionalisation of police is founded on the understanding of the critically important role they have, in partnerships, across the widest range of health and welfare issues, and that if they are adequately paid and trained they will be more amenable to learning new roles and attitudes – and more accountable.

None of this is to be read as excusing adverse police behaviours in relation to people and communities at risk of HIV; rather, without an understanding of the drivers of this behavior, attempts to change it will be unsuccessful.

Creating police allies in the global response to HIV

In our experience, there are three common erroneous strains of thought among many civil society, non-government organisations (NGOs) and agencies involved in the HIV response, which may affect their willingness to work with police:

- that police are merely passive implementers of the law; so that if the law is reformed, police attitudes and behaviours towards most at risk (MAR) communities will automatically fall in line.
- that police are the enemy, and that their behaviours are not amenable to change without confrontation, and/or
- that training and sensitisation of police is adequate to change police behaviour towards MAR communities.

'Police can be your worst enemy, or your best friend' is a truism to the HIV program manager. While in many situations, police are the enemy of a human rights based approach to HIV prevention and care among vulnerable populations, this is not always the case.

In some instances, changes in police behaviours have been in advance of law reform, through partnership with the HIV sector and beneficial exercise of discretion.

Some HIV programs around the world have been able to work with police, rather than against them, to help ameliorate hostile policing practices which are key drivers of HIV risk (among many other risks to MAR communities).

An example of such achievements is a more sensitive approach to patrolling near needle-syringe program outlets, with standard operating procedures in some jurisdictions now recommending no targeting of needle exchanges.

Similarly, in Ghana, police not only stopped harassing women carrying condoms as sex workers, but have begun carrying condoms themselves for distribution to sex workers.[3] Such approaches are by no means universal, but the list of positive examples is growing.[4]

The Global Commission on HIV and the Law clearly recognises the potential positive role of police, and the urgent need to harness this force to the cause of HIV prevention:

'The legal environment – laws, enforcement and justice systems –has immense potential to better the lives of HIV-positive people and to help turn the crisis around.' (p. 7)[5]

'There are instances where legal and justice systems have played constructive roles in responding to HIV, by respecting, protecting and fulfilling human rights. To some such an approach may seem a paradox – the AIDS paradox. But compelling evidence shows that it is the way to reduce the toll of HIV.' (p. 9)[6]

Given this background, LEAHN was established to help build informed, trained and supportive police forces as strong allies in the fight against HIV.

LEAHN provides a crucial infrastructure that connects police to the HIV sector and communicates harm reduction best practice within the domain of law enforcement. In some ways, police and security forces are a hard to reach key population – despite being identifiable through their uniforms, they may not see themselves as 'at-risk' or as important actors in the HIV response.

LEAHN, therefore, plays a dual role: it channels health and safety information among law enforcement officers to prevent transmission risk through needle-stick injury or unsafe sexual behaviours, and acts as a conduit between police and key populations to repair strained relations and build mutually beneficial trust for effective implementation of HIV prevention services.

The Impact of Peers

Culture change in a closed culture is best achieved through peer-led interventions, such as modeling and peer education to create a sustainable and supportive environment, which LEAHN helps to create. Key to LEAHN's success is a network of serving or retired police or law enforcement officers (known as Country Focal Points – CFPs) who provide the impetus to connect to their peers and the HIV sector.[7]

LEAHN is expanding, with 20 CFPs representing different countries. The CFPs have produced a video in which they explain why they see police engagement in the HIV response as critical.[8]

As peers, CFPs are a credible and authoritative source of information about best practice harm reduction approaches, facilitating information sharing between senior and junior officers and specialist and general police.

This work takes place in a range of ways, including training sessions, face-to-face discussions, internal policy review and via social media channels. The CFP cultivates all these opportunities and nurtures the learning process.

The network facilitates information sharing within and across countries, highlighting examples where police and law enforcement have been key partners in harm reduction, and turning examples of best practice into tools which can be used as impetus for police in other countries to adopt harm reduction approaches.

Such examples may even convince non-government organisations that it is worthwhile engaging with police, where it may have otherwise been deemed too difficult or dangerous.

Some police keenly see the benefits of harm reduction and are early adopters of new practices, while others require ongoing persuasion. In the latter case, the LEAHN peer network provides essential infrastructure to buttress messages which challenge ineffective practices and unhelpful norms in order to convince officers to change their old habits.

LEAHN, through its International Police Advisory Group, has published a Statement of Support by police for harm reduction approaches to policing vulnerable populations.[9]

This Statement has been signed by over 10,000 police worldwide, and continues to accrue more support. It was launched by a delegation of police from LEAHN at the UN Commission on Crime Prevention and Criminal Justice in Vienna in April 2013.

It carries a strong message – informing police that this approach is not foreign to policing practices, but is in fact policy among many police agencies already, and has enormous support among police peers and colleagues.

It also informs the HIV community that there are many police ready and willing to engage in a partnership to confront not only HIV but the underlying human rights issues affecting MAR communities.

Conclusion

There is a pressing need for more sustained engagement with police around HIV prevention and care; it needs to be better framed as culture change, and integrated with global movements to professionalise policing.

It is our hope that through the work of LEAHN, HIV health professionals and communities most affected by HIV can work together help to achieve positive change within the police force.

Notes

1. Global Commission on HIV and the Law (2012). HIV and the Law: Risks, Rights and Health. United Nations Development Programme (UNDP), New York. Retrieved from: www.hivlawcommission.org

2. ibid.

3. Open Society Foundations. (2014). To Protect and Serve: How Police, Sex Workers, and People Who Use Drugs Are Joining Forces to Improve Health and Human Rights. Open Society Foundations, New York. Retrieved from: www.opensocietyfoundations. org

4. The LEAHN website lists a number of positive examples of partnerships between law enforcement agencies, governments and NGOs to address HIV epidemics. See: www. leahn.org/police-hiv-programs

5. Global Commission on HIV and the Law. (2012). op. cit., 7.

6. ibid.

7. For further information on LEAHN Country Focal Points see: www.leahn.org/people/country-focal-points

8. Available at: https://youtu.be/KzeBlYVRlYw

9. Law Enforcement and HIV Network (LEAHN). (2013). Statement of Support for Harm Reduction Policing.

| *"Police practices often reflect community prejudices."*

Active Police Engagement Can Help Meet the 2030 Goal to End AIDS

Nick Crofts and David Patterson

In the following viewpoint, excerpted for length, Nick Crofts and David Patterson argue that public health and police must work together to meet the challenge of ending AIDS by 2030. Crofts and Patterson contend professional and personal police interests must be taken into account and aligned for increased engagement to be successful. As an example, they cite emphasizing occupational health and safety issues to garner support for needle and syringe programs. Nick Crofts is Director, Centre for Law Enforcement and Public Health in Melbourne, Australia. David Patterson is Program Manager/Advisor, Health Law for the International Development Law Organization in The Hague, Netherlands.

"Police Must Join the Fast Track to End AIDS by 2030," by Nick Crofts and David Patterson, Journal of the International AIDS Society, July 18, 2016. https://www.ncbi.nlm.nih.gov/pmc/articles/PMC4951534/. Licensed under CC BY 3.0 Unported.

As you read, consider the following questions:

1. Who are responsible for translating the law of the book to the law on the street?

2. What United Kingdom experience is offered here as an example of successful police engagement for HIV response?

3. What four approaches are necessary to reduce stigma?

World leaders have committed to ending AIDS by 2030, but stigma and discrimination remain significant obstacles. In particular, police are critical, front-line determinants of risk for many people living with HIV (PLHIV) and members of other key affected populations (KAPs). The negative impact of adverse police behaviours and practices on HIV risk is well documented, and these risks undermine global efforts to end AIDS. Far less well documented, and less common, are attempts to ameliorate this impact by working to change police behaviours. This Special Issue seeks to help redress this imbalance by presenting a selection of original, provocative and important interventions from academics, police officers and other stakeholders concerned with documenting the potential for constructive, progressive and evidence-based approaches to the reduction of HIV risk. We recommend urgent boosting of efforts and funding to engage police in the HIV response. Among other strategies, this needs sustainable funding of programmes and their evaluation, and increased and continuing advocacy and education at all levels to match policy and law reform.

Introduction

At the Sustainable Development Summit in 2015, world leaders reaffirmed their commitment to end AIDS by 2030. We are at a critical, historical pivot point in the global response. If we do not urgently identify and scale up evidence-based solutions, the human and financial costs of the HIV epidemic will grow into a debt we can never repay [1]. Yet there is one powerful and potentially very useful ally whom we have not adequately engaged in the response—the police. Without the police becoming part of the solution, they will continue to be what they now are in many places, part of the problem, and often a major part. Police engagement in the HIV response is a critical enabler, so why are the police not a leading partner in HIV prevention?

Many people are at risk of acquiring HIV because of socially, and often legally, proscribed behaviours that attract administrative or criminal enforcement practices and sanctions. The responses to such behaviours include detention in so-called "treatment" centres, incarceration and the death penalty, in some countries. Sex work is illegal in more than 100 countries worldwide, and the possession, use and supply of illicit drugs is illegal almost everywhere. Male homosexual behaviour is illegal in 70 countries, punishable by the death penalty in ten. Even where these behaviours are legal, the populations concerned are subject to substantial and varying levels of stigma and discrimination [2].

In all cases, the primary translators of the law on the books to the law on the streets are the police. Even where these behaviours are stigmatized but not illegal, the police, reflecting their communities, are often agents of discrimination. There is a clear connection between discrimination and illegality and the heightened risk for HIV infection among these populations. The behaviours of police are therefore critical in shaping the risk environment for these populations. In many instances, they are overwhelmingly the most important critical determinants of HIV risk [3,4].

Much evidence has been documented of adverse police behaviours towards key affected populations (KAPs), and the adverse impact of these behaviours on HIV risk. Footer et al. have noted the adverse impact on risk behaviours among sex workers [5]. For example, police have been documented in many countries and circumstances as using the possession of condoms as evidence to justify arrest for prostitution. The same is true for needles, syringes and associated injecting paraphernalia. In countries where this police behaviour is common, much of the time the "evidence" is used to extort money, sexual favours, drugs or other bounty. In all instances, the categorization by police of the person as a sex worker, a drug user or a member of a sexual minority provides the apparent rationale for their often inhumane treatment; beating, torture, rape and other human rights abuses are common.

These behaviours have been shown repeatedly to increase the risk of HIV infection and other adverse health consequences [6]. Lunze et al. have documented police violence and HIV risks for female drug users in Russia [7]; Polonsky et al. have noted the links between police harassment, drug addiction and HIV risks among prisoners in Azerbaijan and Kyrgyzstan [8]; and Schneiders and Weissman have reported that laws and their implementation are barriers to HIV prevention, care and treatment in Cambodia [9]. In Ukraine, Kutsa et al. have documented how police practices impede programs for drug users [10]. In South India, Bhattacharjee et al. have reported the HIV risks from police harassment and arrest for sex workers [11]. In response to police behaviours, PLHIV and members of KAPs take their lives underground, leading to circumstances of decreased safety, such as being forced to have or sell sex without the use of a condom, or injecting in haste with used equipment. The police behaviours also preclude or impede access by PLHIV and KAPs to prevention, treatment and care services, and make outreach work difficult, especially outreach undertaken by peers.

Police practices often reflect community prejudices. PLHIV and members of KAPs are in many cultures marginalized, and through a variety of mechanisms, they become the demonized "other." They are treated as outlaws because of their behaviours, and not as full, rights-bearing members of the community. Police may act to protect what they perceive to be their community, the one from which they come, the one they see as legitimate and in conformance with the dominant social and moral norms. The more militarized the police force, the more pronounced this may be, in which case the police may see their role as protecting society

POLICE SUPPORT AND HARM REDUCTION

For harm reduction to work effectively an 'enabling environment' is needed – that is, a whole of community approach must exist where harm reduction is supported by police and other agencies. It is important to note that harm reduction cannot, and will not, work without active support and leadership from police.

There is now greater awareness that the scope of the law enforcement role in addressing drug misuse needs to be more considered, and that in order to reduce the broader range of harms attributed to drug misuse police need to establish effective working relationships with agencies such as health departments and non-government organisations.

Law enforcement agencies are now in a unique position in that police play an important and active role in reducing the impact of drugs in the community through involvement in harm reduction approaches. Police can be extremely effective when they support and actively participate in harm reduction strategies.

Police are aware of their responsibilities and implement policies and practices that help create an enabling environment. Police need to know how they can best support these initiatives that have been designed to address the harms associated with injecting drug use, in particular the spread of HIV.

"Police & HIV Programs," Law Enforcement and Harm Reduction Network.

from the KAPs, who are characterized as internal enemies. Police, thereby, become a key part of the mechanism of discrimination and stigma against these populations.

These outcomes are well proven, which makes it all the more puzzling that changing police behaviours has not been a more prominent goal in programs to address the HIV epidemic in many countries. There has been relatively little documentation of the impact of working with police to change these behaviours, reflecting the relative paucity of such programs. This Special Issue seeks to help redress this imbalance by reporting both problems but also positive interventions seeking constructive, progressive and evidence-based approaches to the reduction of HIV risk.

In part, it would seem that more emphasis has been placed on top-down approaches to law reform, with an implicit belief that police are universally guided by the law and use it impartially. Yet changing the law can take years, whereas changes in policies guiding police practices, and local solutions embedded in local knowledge and relationships involving the police, can be more effective in a much shorter time frame. In the context of treatment for drug dependence, for example, Ma et al. propose testing workable models in local settings, developed by local agencies yet guided by national harm reduction goals and inter-agency collaboration [12].

The Report of the Global Commission on HIV and the Law in 2012 sets out clearly the need for reform of policing practice, recommending that reform of policy and law must go hand-in-hand with reform of law enforcement practices and implementation of policy and law by police [13]. The commission recognized that these are different activities requiring different focuses: achieving reform in one area, law or police does not guarantee concomitant reform in the other, and is achieved by different means.

The Evidence for Police Engagement

The role of law enforcement, especially police, as partners in the public health mission is increasingly well recognized. There is an extensive body of literature going back decades exploring the role of police in public health issues and documenting good models [14]. There is also now an international conference on law enforcement and public health which highlights major public health partnerships in the fields of mental health, gender-based and family violence, road trauma, major events and catastrophes, alcohol-related harm and many other public health issues (www.leph2016.com). If this is the case for other public health issues, why not for HIV? Is it simply because PLHIV and KAPs are so stigmatized, more than almost any other groups in society?

One reason for the failure of AIDS programming to engage police lies in the approach often taken to advocate with police. In effect, the message the police hear is, "Help us do our job, of preventing HIV." The common response is, "That's your job, we've got ours!" often couched in more picturesque terms [15]. For effective advocacy and engagement, we need to look at the issues from the police perspective, something the AIDS research community very rarely does. Leaving aside the issue of corruption, police imperatives are all around crime control and public order and safety, and dialogues about public health or human rights imperatives often have no impact. For advocacy to work, we need to identify and align our approaches to the police interests, both personal and professional [16]. For instance, for the former, some programs have used an approach highlighting occupational health and safety issues as a way to mobilize police support for needle and syringe programs [17]. Occupational health approaches can deliver immediate benefits for both police and public health. As noted by Mittal et al., ceasing syringe confiscation can reduce occupational exposure and limit the sharing of injection equipment among drug users [18]. And as an example of the latter, the introduction of methadone maintenance in Viet Nam won more support and was more successful when police became aware of the crime-control aspects of moving heroin users onto long-term substitution therapy [15,19].

There have been many calls for an end to the police harassment and brutalization of KAPS [20], and for police to protect the health and rights of PLHIV and members of KAPs as much as those of other members of society [21]. There are now increasing calls for maximizing the opportunity to recruit police as partners, facilitators and even leaders in HIV prevention strategies, as exemplified by Polonsky et al.[8]:

> Rather than target [people who inject drugs] for arrest, police could align their practices with public health and steer them towards evidence-based treatment with methadone or buprenorphine ... and help avoid incarceration. Alternatively,

... they can encourage the use [needle and syringe programs] that also reduce HIV risk.

How can we best bring about this change, which is happening or already has in some police agencies worldwide?

There are examples of good practice in relation to police engagement in the HIV response; this is especially the case in high-income countries with democratized police agencies. The United Kingdom's guidance to police on needle and syringe programs is an excellent example of police, prosecutions and public health collaboration in the public interest [22].

Increasingly, the effectiveness of collaborative programs in which the police address discrimination, stigma and HIV risk are being documented in low and middle income countries as well [23]. (The LEAHN website lists a number of positive examples of partnerships between law enforcement agencies, governments and NGOs to address HIV epidemics. See: www.leahn.org/police-hiv-programs.) For instance, the Gates Foundation funds the Avahan program that provides support for work with police in the six Indian states that includes training for police, instructions to police not to use condoms as evidence and support of police for prevention staff [24]. The Poro Sapot project in Papua New Guinea worked to reduce the harassment of men who have sex with men and sex workers through training and sensitization of police at multiple levels [25]. Thomson et al. have reported on a series of joint workshops between police and KAPS supported by the UN Office on Drugs and Crime (UNODC), contributing to the evidence that contact between police and KAPs outside the usual situations of conflict can be effective in rehumanizing each to the other [26]. This aligns with the evidence about what works in stigma reduction, with four approaches necessary and effective: information-based approaches, skills building, counselling and support and contact with affected groups [27]. Specifically, it is more difficult for a police officer to harass a sex worker who the previous day had been playing football with him [23]. Landsberg et al. have concluded that their findings indicate "that a major shift towards a public health approach to policing is possible among a municipal police force" [28]. But it is clearly necessary to strengthen civil society at the same time so as to promote a respectful partnership [7].

[...]

Notes

1. UNAIDS. 2016–2021 strategy: on the fast track to end AIDS. Geneva: UNAIDS; 2016.

2. UNAIDS. The gap report. Geneva: UNAIDS; 2014.

3. Burris S, Blankenship KM, Donoghoe M, Sherman S, Vernick JS, Case P, et al. Addressing the "Risk Environment" for injection drug users: the mysterious case of the missing cop. Milbank Q. 2004:125–56. [PMC free article] [PubMed]

4. Clark F. Discrimination against LGBT people triggers health concerns. Lancet. 2014;383(9916):500–2.

5. Footer KHA, Silberzahn BE, Tormohlen KN, Sherman SG. Policing practices as a structural determinant for HIV among sex workers: a systematic review of empirical findings. J Int AIDS Soc. 2016;19(Suppl 3) 20883, doi: http://dx.doi.org/10.7448/IAS.19.4.20883.

6. Beletsky L, Thomas R, Smelyanskaya M, Artamonova I, Shumskaya N, Dooronbekova A, et al. Policy reform to shift the health and human rights environment for vulnerable groups: the case of Kyrgyzstan's Instruction 417. Health Hum Right. 2012;14(2):1–5.

7. Lunze K, Raj A, Cheng DM, Quinn EK, Lunze FI, Liebschutz JM, et al. Sexual violence from police and HIV risk behaviours among HIV-positive women who inject drugs in St. Petersburg, Russia – a mixed methods study. J Int AIDS Soc. 2016;19(Suppl 3) 20877, doi: http://dx.doi.org/10.7448/IAS.19.4.20877.

8. Polonsky M, Azbel L, Wegman MP, Izenberg JM, Bachireddy C, Wickersham JA, et al. Pre-incarceration police harassment, drug addiction and HIV risk behaviours among prisoners in Kyrgyzstan and Azerbaijan: results from a nationally representative cross-sectional study. J Int AIDS Soc. 2016;19(Suppl 3) 20880, doi: http://dx.doi.org/10.7448/IAS.19.4.20880.

9. Schneiders ML, Weissman A. Determining barriers to creating an enabling environment in Cambodia: results from a baseline study with key populations and police. J Int AIDS Soc. 2016;19(Suppl 3) 20878, doi: http://dx.doi.org/10.7448/IAS.19.4.20878.

10. Kutsa O, Marcus R, Bojko MJ, Zelenev A, Mazhnaya A, Dvoriak S, et al. Factors associated with physical and sexual violence by police among people who inject drugs in Ukraine: implications for retention on opioid agonist therapy. J Int AIDS Soc. 2016;19(Suppl 3) 20897, doi: http://dx.doi.org/10.7448/IAS.19.4.20897.

11. Bhattacharjee P, Isac S, McClarty LM, Mohan HL, Maddur S, Jagannath SB, et al. Strategies for reducing police arrest in the context of an HIV prevention programme for female sex workers: evidence from structural interventions in Karnataka, South India. J Int AIDS Soc. 2016;19(Suppl 3) 20856, doi: http://dx.doi.org/10.7448/IAS.19.4.20856.

12. Ma Y, Du C, Cai T, Han Q, Yuan H, Luo T, et al. Barriers to community-based drug dependence treatment: implications for police roles, collaborations and performance indicators. J Int AIDS Soc. 2016;19(Suppl 3) 20879, doi: http://dx.doi.org/10.7448/IAS.19.4.20879.

13. Global Commission on HIV and the law. HIV and the law: risks, rights and health [Internet] New York: United Nations Development Programme; 2012.

14. Punch M. The secret social service. In: Holdaway S, editor. The British Police. London: Arnold; 1979. pp. 102–17.

15. LEHRN Partnership. Sleeping with the enemy? Engaging with law enforcement in prevention of HIV among and from injecting drug users in Asia. HIV Matters. 2010;2(1):14–16.

16. Reiner R. The politics of the police. 4th edn. Oxford: Oxford University Press; 2010.

17. Beletsky L, Macalino G, Burris S. Attitudes of police officers towards syringe access, occupational needle-sticks and drug use: a qualitative study of one city police department in the United States. Int J Drug Policy. 2005;16:267–74.

18. Mittal ML, Patiño E, Beletsky L, Abramovitz D, Rocha T, Arredondo J, et al. Prevalence and correlates of needle-stick injuries among active duty police officers in Tijuana, Mexico. J Int AIDS Soc. 2016;19(Suppl 3) 20874, doi: http://dx.doi.org/10.7448/IAS.19.4.20874.

19. Jardine M, Crofts N, Morrow M, Monaghan G. Harm reduction and law enforcement in Vietnam: influences on street policing. Harm Reduction J. 2012;9(27):1–5.

20. Godwin J. Laws affecting HIV responses among men who have sex with men and transgender persons in Asia and the Pacific: an agenda for action. Bangkok, Thailand: UN Development Programme; 2010.

21. Shaw SY, Lorway RR, Deering KN, Avery L, Mohan HL, Bhattacharjee P, et al. Factors associated with sexual violence against men who have sex with men and transgendered individuals in Karnataka, India. PLoS One. 2012;7(3):e31705.

22. Crown Prosecution Service (UK) Prosecution policy and guidance: legal guidance: drug offences (undated) [Internet] [cited 2016 Mar 21]. Available from http://www.cps.gov.uk/

23. Open Society Foundations (OSF) New York: Open Society Foundations; 2014. To protect and serve: how police, sex workers, and people who use drugs are joining forces to improve health and human rights [Internet]

24. Biradavolu MR, Burris S, George A, Jena A, Blankenship KM. Can sex workers regulate police? Learning from an HIV prevention project for sex workers in southern India. Soc Sci Med. 2009;68(8):1541–7.

25. Maibani-Michie G, Kavanamur D, Jikian M, Siba P. Evaluation of the Poro Sapot Project: intervention-linked baseline and post-intervention studies. Goroka: Papua New Guinea Institute of Medical Research; 2007.

26. Thomson N, Riley D, Bergenstrom A, Carpenter J, Zelitchenko A. From conflict to partnership: growing collaboration between police and NGOs in countries with concentrated epidemics among key populations. J Int AIDS Soc. 2016;19(Suppl 3) 20939, doi: http://dx.doi.org/10.7448/IAS.19.4.20939.

27. Brown L, Macintyre K, Trujillo L. Interventions to reduce HIV/AIDS stigma: what have we learned? AIDS Educ Prev. 2003;15(1):49–69. [PubMed]

28. Landsberg A, Kerr T, Milloy M-J, Dong H, Nguyen P, Wood E, et al. Declining trends in exposures to harmful policing among people who inject drugs in Vancouver, Canada. J Int AIDS Soc. 2016;19(Suppl 3) 20729, doi: http://dx.doi.org/10.7448/IAS.19.4.20729.

> *"The risk of serious harm to other persons or property is the most commonly asserted and well-accepted justification for public health regulation."*

Safeguarding Public Health Through the Law

Lawrence O. Gostin and Lindsay F. Wiley

In the following viewpoint, Lawrence Gostin and Lindsay Wiley argue that the law can be an effective tool for protecting public health. They posit that the public good must be weighed against individual liberty and bodily integrity. Lawrence Gostin is the Founding O'Neill Chair in Global Health Law and Director of the O'Neill Institute for National and Global Health Law and the World Health Organization Collaborating Center on Public Health Law and Human Rights at Georgetown University. He is also professor of public health at Johns Hopkins University. Lindsay Wiley is associate professor of the Washington College of Law at American University in Washington, DC.

"Public Health Ethics and Law," by Lawrence O. Gostin and Lindsay F. Wiley, The Hastings Center Bioethics Briefings. Reprinted by permission.

As you read, consider the following questions:

1. What are the three general areas for public health focus?
2. What four ethical questions do public health practitioners need to grapple with, according to this viewpoint?
3. According to this viewpoint, do laws need reform to deal with syringe programs?

The role of public health is to assure the conditions needed to promote and protect people's health. These conditions include various economic, social, and environmental factors that are necessary for good health. The Institute of Medicine (IOM) defines public health as "what we, as a society, do collectively to assure the conditions for people to be healthy." With its use of the phrase "we, as a society," the IOM emphasizes cooperative and mutually shared obligation. It also reinforces the notion that collective entities (e.g., governments and communities) are responsible for healthy populations. This idea is critical because the political community does not have a clear sense of the concept of public health apart from the discourse around health care reform. Efforts to assure access to high-quality health care are certainly an important part of improving the public's health, but they play a relatively minor role compared to broader efforts to assure equitable access to healthy living conditions.

Today, public health is more important than ever. Society faces threats from emerging and resurgent infectious diseases such as Zika virus, declining vaccination rates, antimicrobial resistance, and the threat of bioterrorism (for example, from anthrax and smallpox). At the same time, public health law and ethics are evolving to address the mounting burdens of noncommunicable disease such as cancer, cardiovascular disease, diabetes, and chronic respiratory disease, injuries or deaths (for example, related to drug overdose, guns, and motor vehicles), and the social determinants of health (for example, the impact of household income, community resources, and structural racism on population health). Efforts to address these burdens more broadly prompt political opposition from people who would prefer a narrower scope for public health law. Others argue that it would be unethical, in the face of preventable morbidity and mortality, to confine the focus of public health to narrowly-defined collective action problems and market failures.

Ethical Values in Tension

Public health regulation often involves potential trade-offs between public goods and private interests. When public health officials act, they face troubling conflicts between the collective benefits of population health on the one hand and personal and economic interests on the other. Public health regulation is designed to monitor health threats and intervene to reduce risk or ameliorate harm within the population. At the same time, public health powers may encroach on fundamental civil liberties such as privacy, bodily integrity, and freedom of movement, association, religion, or expression. Sanitary regulations may also intrude on basic economic liberties such as freedom of contract, pursuit of professional status, use of property, and competitive markets.

Although, undoubtedly, there are tensions between individual and collective interests, there are also synergies. The protection of civil liberties may improve population health. For example, privacy and antidiscrimination protections for individuals with stigmatized conditions may encourage them to seek testing, counseling, and treatment. When public health measures are designed to protect civil rights and liberties they are more likely to benefit from the earned trust and cooperation of the community and, in particular, persons at risk.

The fields of bioethics and medical ethics have richly informed the development and use of biotechnologies, the practice of medicine, and the allocation of health care resources. If a single overarching principle could be extrapolated from these traditions, it is that individuals have a strong claim to make decisions for themselves, at least to the extent that those decisions are purely self-regarding without imposing consequences on others. Thus, if a person has the capacity to understand the nature and consequences of the decision at hand, she has an interest in making her own choice without outside interference. Autonomy is a guiding value that supports a constellation of individual rights to, for example, confidentiality, informed consent, and liberty.

Bioethics, because of the premium it places on individual rights, has had limited relevance to the ethical dilemmas of public health, which often involve balancing individual rights against the needs of the community as a whole. Under the public health tradition, individual interests may have to yield to those of the broader community when necessary for the public's health, safety, and well-being. The public health tradition values prevention and views its successes or failures based on the benefits and burdens that accrue to populations rather than to individuals.

In recent years, however, several bioethics scholars have begun to give more attention to principles of social justice in response to problems such as universal access to health care and social disparities in health. At the same time, public health ethics has emerged as a distinct field in its own right, with attention to the professional ethics of public health practitioners and the applied ethics of public health policymaking. While virtually every aspect of public health research, practice, and policy raises issues that call for ethical analysis, there are three general areas on which the emerging field of public health ethics has been particularly focused: the role of values in risk assessment, public health paternalism, and social disparities in health.

Risk Assessment

How should policy-makers respond to the public's lack of scientific understanding of risk? Should public perceptions be understood to reflect values worthy of balancing alongside the scientific risk assessments of experts? Or should they be treated as irrationalities to be corrected (through education programs) or circumvented (through reliance on expertise-driven administrative agencies insulated from democratic accountability)?

Public Health Paternalism

The risk of serious harm to other persons or property is the most commonly asserted and well-accepted justification for public health regulation. Even those who advocate for the minimal use of state powers endorse infectious disease control measures that limit liberty (e.g., mandatory vaccination, physical examination, treatment, isolation of the infected and quarantine of the exposed), at least in high-risk circumstances such as an outbreak of Ebola virus. The "harm principle" in bioethics holds that competent adults should have freedom of action unless they pose a risk to others. In competent individuals, harm to self or immoral conduct is insufficient to justify state action. Consequently, "risk to self" is a much more controversial justification for public health regulation.

Paternalism is the intentional interference with a person's freedom of action exclusively—or primarily—to protect his or her own health, safety, welfare, or happiness. Longstanding regulation of behavior that poses a risk to one's self includes mandatory motorcycle helmet and seat belt laws, gambling prohibitions, and criminalization of recreational drugs. More recently, restrictions on tobacco, fast food, and sugary drink manufacturers and retailers have riled critics who claim these actions invoke a public health "nanny state."

Opponents of paternalism value freedom of choice, arguing that individuals should be allowed to decide for themselves, even if they make what experts might deem the "unhealthy" or "unsafe" choice. Supporters of paternalism point out that there are both internal and external constraints on people's capacity to pursue their own interests. Personal behavior is not simply a matter of free will. So, state regulation is sometimes necessary to protect an individual's health or safety. For example, everyone does not know that children are at risk of severe injury from front-seat air bags or that radon is prevalent and dangerous in homes. Even when information is available, consumers may misapprehend the risks. And advertising can persuade consumers to make unhealthy decisions about tobacco, alcoholic beverages, sugary drinks, or high-calorie food.

Perhaps it is more accurate to think of public health paternalism as directed towards overall societal welfare rather than the individual. Public health policy is aimed at the community and measures its success by improved population health and longevity. Even if conduct is primarily self-regarding, the aggregate effects of persons choosing not to wear seatbelts or helmets can be thousands of preventable injuries and deaths. Thus, while risk-to-self is often the least politically acceptable reason for regulation, it is nonetheless clear that paternalistic policies can be effective in preventing injuries and deaths in the population.

Health Disparities and Social Justice
Social justice is so central to the mission of public health that it is often described as the field's core value. One the most basic and commonly understood principles of justice is that individuals and groups should receive fair, equitable, and appropriate treatment in light of what is due or owed to them. Justice, for example, can offer guidance on how to allocate scarce therapeutic resources in a public health crisis, such as pandemic influenza.

Social justice, however, demands more than merely a fair distribution of resources. While health hazards threaten the entire population, the poor and disabled are at heightened risk. For example, in response to devastating hurricanes on the Gulf Coast in 2005 and the East Coast in 2011 and 2012, city, state, and federal agencies failed to act expeditiously and with equal concern for all citizens, particularly the poor and disabled. Neglect of the needs of the vulnerable predictably harms the whole community by eroding public trust and undermining social cohesion. Social justice thus encompasses not only a core commitment to a fair distribution of resources, but it also calls for policies of action that are consistent with the preservation of human dignity and the showing of equal respect for the interests of all members of the community.

Law and Public Health Ethics

Public health practice and ethics are intimately intertwined with public health law, which shapes the authority of the state to protect the public's health and limits that power in the form of individual rights and structural constraints. As Daniel Callahan and Bruce Jennings have noted, "[p]ublic health is one of the few professions that has, in many matters, legal power–in particular, the police power of the state–behind it. . . . It thus has an obligation both toward government, which controls it, and toward the public that it serves."

Many of the most important social and ethical debates about public health take place in legal forums–legislatures, courts, and administrative agencies–and in the law's language of rights, duties, and justice. Law defines the jurisdiction of public health officials and specifies the manner in which they may exercise their authority. State public health statutes create public health agencies, designate their mission and core functions, appropriate their funds, grant their power, and limit their actions to protect certain liberties.

The law can be an effective tool for safeguarding the public's health. Of the 10 greatest public health achievements of the twentieth century, all were realized, at least in part, through legal reform or litigation: vaccinations, safer workplaces, safer and healthier foods, motor vehicle safety, control of infectious diseases, the decline in deaths from coronary heart disease and stroke, family planning, tobacco control, healthier mothers and babies, and fluoridation of drinking water. Public health law experts are playing a vital role in addressing the leading public health challenges of the twenty-first century. Their efforts include creating a more rational, accessible health care system; eliminating health disparities among racial and ethnic groups; integrating physical activity and healthy eating into everyday life; protecting the natural environment; and, responding to emerging and reemerging infectious diseases. Public health law consists of the basic statutes that empower public health agencies and a number of legal tools, including:

- Taxation and spending. Taxes can provide incentives for healthy behaviors (such as deductions for health insurance) and disincentives for risk behaviors (for example, excise taxes on tobacco products and sugary drinks). Spending can directly support public health infrastructure and healthy living conditions, or it can be conditioned on compliance with health-promoting regulations (such as safety standards for the receipt of highway funds and nutrition standards for food served in public schools).
- The information environment. Government can educate the public, require labeling of food, drugs, tobacco, and other hazardous products, and regulate advertising (for example, restricting ads that target children).
- The built environment. Government can use zoning and planning authority to help individuals to make healthy choices (for example, reducing the concentration of fast food, firearm, liquor, or gambling outlets and investing in public transportation, parks, bicycle paths, and recreational facilities).
- The socioeconomic environment. Government can allocate resources and create policies to reduce the vast inequalities in health related to socioeconomic status, race, ethnicity, or geography by supporting access to housing, education, and income.
- Direct regulation. Government can directly regulate individuals (such as by imposing travel restrictions or mandating vaccination to control infectious disease), businesses (such as by requiring calorie counts on restaurant menus), and professionals (such as by imposing health and safety regulation on health care professionals and others via licensing authority).
- Indirect regulation through the tort system. Attorneys and private citizens can use civil litigation to redress many different kinds of public health harms relating to the

environment (such as air or water pollution), toxic substances (such as pesticides or radiation), hazardous products (such as tobacco or firearms), and defective consumer products.

- Deregulation. Sometimes laws need to be reformed because they pose an obstacle to the public's health –for example, prohibitions against distribution of sterile injection equipment to illicit drug users as part of HIV/AIDS prevention programs.

On the Horizon

The United States faces many formidable challenges in safeguarding the population from infectious and noncommunicable diseases and injuries. The mounting toll of Type 2 diabetes, dramatically rising rates of opioid overdose, outbreaks of measles and pertussis, and Zika virus transmission brings ethical values into tension. The duty to protect the public–a collective good–must be weighed against individual rights to liberty, privacy, bodily integrity, freedom of association, and the free exercise of religion. In view of these competing values, public health practitioners are grappling with several critical questions:

- What limits on privacy are justified by surveillance, and to what extent does the answer depend on whether officials are tracking noncommunicable conditions or injuries as opposed to communicable diseases?
- What limits on bodily integrity are justified by screening, physical examination, and treatment?
- What limits on liberty are justified by quarantine and social distancing measures designed to separate the healthy from those infected or exposed to communicable disease?
- What limits on individual rights are justified by mandatory vaccination against preventable illnesses?

When facing the public health challenges of coming decades, policy makers will be unable to avoid ethical dilemmas. Failure to move aggressively–even with incomplete scientific information–

can have disastrous consequences, while actions that prove to have been unnecessary will be viewed as draconian and wasteful. Transparency is crucial. Policymakers must be willing not only to clearly explain the reasons for restrictive measures, but also to openly acknowledge when new evidence warrants a reconsideration of policies. Potential interventions must be evaluated according to carefully honed ethical criteria. In the future as in the past, public health decisions will profoundly reflect the manner in which societies both implicitly and explicitly balance values that are intimately related and inherently in tension.

> "*Much federal funding for
> treatment is, in fact, funneled
> into the criminal justice system—
> which is far less effective than
> health-based approaches.*"

The Federal Government Budget for the 21ˢᵗ Century Should Invest in Drug Treatment and Prevention

Drug Policy Alliance

In the following viewpoint, specialists at the Drug Policy Alliance argue that the federal government spends more money on incarceration than in establishing educational programs. It finds that the federal government favors abstinence-only strategies over evidence-based harm reduction strategies. The Alliance calls for a non-partisan approach to invest government dollars in quality treatment programs that optimizes the federal budget. The Drug Policy Alliance is a New York City-based organization whose mission is to promote drug harm reduction policies as well as to promote individual control over mind and body.

"The Federal Drug Control Budget," Drug Policy Alliance, February 2015. Reprinted by permission.

As you read, consider the following questions:

1. According to this viewpoint, did the Obama administration want to treat drug use as a health issue or a criminal justice issue?
2. How much of the 2016 federal budget targeted demand reduction? Harm reduction?
3. According to this viewpoint, what have the federal budget and drug policies focused on?

The Obama administration says that drug use should be treated as a health issue instead of a criminal justice issue. Yet its budget and its drug policies have largely emphasized enforcement, prosecution and incarceration at home, and interdiction, eradication and military escalation abroad. Even what the government does spend on treatment and prevention is overstated, as many of its programs are wasteful and counterproductive.

Drug War Policies Dominate Federal Drug Budget

The enacted federal drug war budget totaled roughly $26 billion in 2015, and the Office of National Drug Control Policy (ONDCP) has requested an even larger budget for 2016.[1] An additional $25 billion is spent at the state and local levels on the drug war every year.[2]

A significant majority of this annual budget—roughly 55 percent —is devoted to policies that attempt to reduce the supply of drugs, such as interdiction, eradication and domestic law enforcement. Less than 45 percent is devoted to treatment, education and prevention—what is commonly known as "demand reduction." Almost nothing is spent on life-saving harm reduction services.

Treatment and education programs are far more effective than arrests and incarceration.

The 2016 budget request is not much different. It contains nearly the same basic ratio of supply-to-demand funding. These distorted funding priorities have not changed significantly under the last several administrations.

ONDCP

The Office of National Drug Control Policy (ONDCP) works to reduce drug use and its consequences by leading and coordinating the development, implementation, and assessment of U.S. drug policy. In addition to its vital ongoing work, ONDCP also provides administrative and financial support to the President's Commission on Combating Drug Addiction and the Opioid Crisis, established by Executive Order on March 29, 2017 by President Donald J. Trump.

A component of the Executive Office of the President, ONDCP was created by the Anti-Drug Abuse Act of 1988. The ONDCP Director is the principal advisor to the President on drug control issues. ONDCP coordinates the drug control activities and related funding of 16 Federal Departments and Agencies. Each year, ONDCP produces the annual National Drug Control Strategy, which outlines Administration efforts for the Nation to reduce illicit drug use, manufacturing and trafficking; drug-related crime and violence; and drug-related health consequences. ONDCP also leads the development of the consolidated Federal drug control budget, which is published annually in the National Drug Control Strategy: Budget and Performance Summary. The FY 2017 budget request for drug control funding is $31.4 billion. ONDCP also administers two grant programs: the High Intensity Drug Trafficking Areas (HIDTA) and Drug-Free Communities (DFC).

"Office of National Drug Control Policy," The White House.

Supply reduction efforts have proven ineffective, costly and destructive, and have distracted from proven strategies to reduce the harms of drug misuse. Despite incarcerating tens of millions of people and spending more than a trillion dollars in the past forty years,[3] drugs remain cheap, potent and widely available.[4]

The drug war strategy also pulls any discussion of alternatives to failed prohibitionist policies off the table. While President Obama and other members of his administration have gone so far as to say that drug legalization is a legitimate topic for debate, the administration's drug control strategies have disparaged marijuana regulation.[5]

Demand Reduction: Underfunded and Overstated

The federal government simply refuses to prioritize proven demand reduction strategies, even though the U.S. is the largest consumer of drugs in the world. Effective treatment and education programs are a far better investment—and far more likely to improve public safety and health—than arrests and incarceration. A seminal study by the RAND Corporation found that every dollar invested in drug treatment saves taxpayers $7.46 in societal costs—a reduction that would cost 15 times as much in supply- side, law enforcement expenditure to achieve.[6]

Even what the government does spend on demand reduction is overstated, because many of these programs have been wasteful and unsuccessful. For example, several longstanding federal prevention efforts, like the National Youth Anti-Drug Media campaign[7] and Drug Abuse Resistance Education (DARE) program[8]—are costly, ineffective, and might actually lead to unintended negative consequences.

Much federal funding for treatment is, in fact, funneled into the criminal justice system – which is far less effective than health-based approaches. Drug courts, have not significantly reduced the likelihood of incarceration, routinely deny proven treatments like methadone, and absorb scarce resources better spent on demonstrated health approaches like community- based treatment.[9] It's disingenuous for ONDCP to claim that wasting money on failed, criminal justice approaches is "treatment". It is not.

The biggest problem we face isn't the use of drugs; it's the misuse of drugs. Data consistently show that the vast majority of people who experiment with illegal drugs do not develop addiction or dependence.

Arresting people who use drugs non-problematically and forcing them into treatment takes up resources that could be invested in helping people struggling with serious drug problems. People who use marijuana are much less likely to become dependent but are increasingly forced into treatment by the criminal justice system—the source of over half of all treatment referrals for marijuana each year.[10] Forcing people into treatment instead of prison for low-level drug offenses is definitely not a health approach. Getting arrested should not be a requirement for receiving treatment.

The federal government continues to privilege abstinence-only approaches to treatment and prevention, to the exclusion of proven, evidence-based interventions. This costly, punitive, zero-tolerance approach has overwhelmingly failed. The U.S. Government Accountability Office (GAO) found that ONDCP has "not made progress toward achieving most of the goals articulated in the 2010 National Drug Control Strategy," and, in fact, has lost ground in vital areas like reducing youth drug use, overdose deaths, and HIV infections among people who inject drugs.[11]

Conclusion

President Obama and members of his administration say that drug use should be treated as a health issue, not a criminal justice issue.[12] The administration has even adopted some limited drug policy changes: pledging not to interfere with states that regulate marijuana and embracing certain overdose prevention and sentencing reform measures, such as de- emphasizing the federal prosecution of low-level drug offenses to reduce federal prison overcrowding.[13]

Yet his budget and the bulk of his drug policies continue to emphasize enforcement, prosecution and incarceration at home, and interdiction, eradication and military escalation abroad.

After 40 years of failure, we need to invest in proven health-based strategies—not just talk about them. Instead of throwing more money at supply-side interventions that are proven failures, the Drug Policy Alliance advocates addressing U.S. demand for drugs by funding a diverse array of treatment models and effective prevention and harm reduction programs.[14]

It's time we developed a comprehensive strategy for dealing with drug abuse in the 21st century by focusing on what works. We know what doesn't work: In the last 30 years, the number of

Americans in prison has increased tenfold. We have less than 5% of the world's population but almost 25% of its prison population. This isn't a partisan issue. Facing massive budget deficits, both parties are searching for alternatives to prison for people who use drugs—because locking them up is only making us poorer, not safer.

But thanks to decades of scientific research, we now know a lot about what does work. We know, for example, that every dollar spent on quality treatment for drug-dependent people returns several dollars in savings in the first year alone. It's time we treated people struggling with drug misuse the way we'd want to help a family member struggling with addiction to alcohol or other drugs: by using what works.

Notes

1. White House Office of National Drug Control Policy, "National Drug Control Budget: Fy2016 Funding Highlights," (Washington, DC: Office of National Drug Control Policy, 2015).

2. Jeffrey A Miron and Katherine Waldock, The Budgetary Impact of Ending Drug Prohibition (Cato Institute, 2010).

3. Martha Mendoza, "Us Drug War Has Met None of Its Goals," AP, May 13(2010).

4. Dan Werb et al., "The Temporal Relationship between Drug Supply Indicators: An Audit of International Government Surveillance Systems," BMJ Open 3, no. 9 (2013); Jonathan P Caulkins and Peter Reuter, "How Drug Enforcement Affects Drug Prices," Crime and Justice 39, no. 1 (2010); C. Costa Storti and P. De Grauwe, "The Cocaine and Heroin Markets in the Era of Globalisation and Drug Reduction Policies," Int J Drug Policy 20, no. 6 (2009); A. Fries et al., "The Price and Purity of Illicit Drugs: 1981-2007," (DTIC Document, 2008).

5. "2013 National Drug Control Strategy," (Washington, DC: Office of National Drug Control Policy, 2013); "2012 National Drug Control Strategy," (Washington, DC: Office of National Drug Control Policy, 2012).

6. C Peter Rydell and Susan S Everingham, Controlling Cocaine: Supply Versus Demand Programs, vol. 331 (Rand Corporation, 1994).

7. Government Accountability Office, Contractor's National Evaluation Did Not Find That the Youth Anti-Drug Media Campaign Was Effective in Reducing Youth Drug Use, (August 2006); R. Hornik and L. Jacobsohn, "The Best Laid Plans: Disappointments of the National Youth Anti-Drug Media Campaign," LDI Issue Brief 14, no. 2 (2008); R. Hornik et al., "Effects of the National Youth Anti-Drug Media Campaign on Youths," Am J Public Health 98, no. 12 (2008).

8. Stephen R. Shamblen et al., "A Short-Term, Quasi-Experimental Evaluation of D.A.R.E.'S Revised Elementary School Curriculum," Journal of Drug Education 40, no. 1 (2010); Marjorie E Kanof, "Youth Illicit Drug Use Prevention: Dare Long-Term

Evaluations and Federal Efforts to Identify Effective Programs," (Washington D.C.: Government Accountability Office, 2003); S. L. West and K. K. O'Neal, "Project D.A.R.E. Outcome Effectiveness Revisited," Am J Public Health 94, no. 6 (2004); Mary Nakashian, "A New Dare Curriculum Gets Mixed Reviews: Communications Activities for Improving and Evaluating the Dare School-Based Substance Abuse Prevention Curriculum. Program Results Report," Robert Wood Johnson Foundation (2010).

9. Drug Policy Alliance, Drug Courts Are Not the Answer: Toward a Health- Centered Approach to Drug Use (Drug Policy Alliance, 2011); Nastassia Walsh, "Addicted to Courts: How a Growing Dependence on Drug Courts Impacts People and Communities," (Justice Policy Institute, 2011); Eric L. Sevigny, Harold A. Pollack, and Peter Reuter, "Can Drug Courts Help to Reduce Prison and Jail Populations?," The Annals of the American Academy of Political and Social Science 647, no. 1 (2013); H. Matusow et al., "Medication Assisted Treatment in Us Drug Courts: Results from a Nationwide Survey of Availability, Barriers and Attitudes," J Subst Abuse Treat (2012).

10. Substance Abuse and Mental Health Services Administration, "National Survey of Substance Abuse Treatment Services (N-Ssats): 2011 Data," (Rockville, MD: Substance Abuse and Mental Health Services Administration, 2013).

11. Government Accountability Office, Office of National Drug Control Policy: Office Could Better Identify Opportunities to Increase Program Coordination (Washington, DC: United States Government Accountability Office, 2013).

12. David Morgan, "Data suggests drug treatment can lower U.S. crime," Reuters (May 17, 2012).) See also, Dan Glaister, "Obama drops 'war on drugs' rhetoric for needle exchanges," The Guardian (March 16, 2009); Rafael Lemaitre to ONDCP Blog, 2014, http://www.whitehouse.gov/blog/2014/01/17/what-does-new-budget- deal-mean-drug-policy-reform.

13. Eric Holder, "Remarks at the Annual Meeting of the American Bar Association's House of Delegates, San Francisco, August 12, 2013," (Office of the Attorney General, United States Department of Justice, 2013).http://www.justice.gov/iso/opa/ag/speeches/2013/ ag-speech-130812.htm; "Memorandum to United States Attorneys: Department Policy on Charging Mandatory Minimum Sentences and Recidivist Enhancements in Certain Drug Cases," (Washington, D.C.: Office of the Attorney General, United States Department of Justice, 2013); James Cole, "Memorandum for All United States Attorneys: Guidance Regarding Marijuana Enforcement," (Washington, DC: U.S. Department of Justice, Office of the Deputy Attorney General, 2013).

> *"The reduction of harm from drug use is the declared purpose for the creation of varied medical and social service facilities."*

Countries Vary in Their Approaches to Narcotics Decriminalization and Harm Reduction Treatments

The Library of Congress

In the following viewpoint, the Library of Congress foreign law specialists argue through their review of narcotics legalization and decriminalization laws in sixteen countries that a variety of approaches exist regarding the prosecution of drug use, possession, production, sale, and purchase. Of particular note is the stance among some countries toward mandatory treatment for those found in possession of illegal substances. In some countries, the accused can choose treatment instead of punishment. The Library of Congress was founded in 1800 and serves the needs of Congress. It is the largest library in the United States.

"Decriminalization of Narcotics: Comparative Summary," The Library of Congress, July 2016. Reprinted by permission.

As you read, consider the following questions:

1. Which countries' laws did the Library of Congress consider for this comparative report?
2. Which countries allow treatment and alternative punishments for minor drug offenses?
3. What is considered a "hard" drug and a "soft" drug?

This report, prepared by the foreign law specialists and analysts of the Law Library of Congress, provides a review of laws adopted in Argentina, Australia, Brazil, Canada, Costa Rica, the Czech Republic, Germany, Ireland, Israel, Mexico, the Netherlands, New Zealand, Norway, Portugal, South Africa, and Uruguay with regard to legalization, decriminalization, or other forms of regulation of narcotics and other psychoactive substances. Individual country surveys included in this study demonstrate varied approaches to the problem of prosecuting drug use, possession, manufacturing, purchase, and sale.

The country surveys demonstrate some diversity and common threads among these jurisdictions as to defining narcotics, distinguishing between "hard" and "soft" drugs, establishing special regulations concerning cannabis, refusing to prosecute personal use and/or possession of small quantities of drugs for personal use, giving law enforcement authorities the discretion not to prosecute minors and first-time offenders, applying alternative forms of punishment, and providing treatment opportunities. The following approaches toward decriminalization of narcotics were identified:

- Production, marketing, and consumption of marijuana is legalized and regulated (Uruguay);
- Drugs are prohibited but the sale and use of soft drugs is tolerated and regulated (Netherlands);
- The personal possession and use of small amounts of drugs is not penalized while other drug-related activities are

prohibited (Costa Rica, Czech Republic, Mexico, Portugal); and

- Treatment and alternative punishments for minor drug offenses are allowed (Argentina, Australia, Brazil, Germany, Israel, New Zealand, Norway).

While most of the countries reviewed do not prosecute individual drug users or have an option for avoiding their criminal prosecution, in general, possessing, manufacturing, and trading in drugs is prohibited. The Czech Republic made the possession of drugs legal after the collapse of the Communist regime but reinstated the penalties for possession in "larger than small" amounts shortly thereafter.

Most of the countries differentiate between soft and hard drugs, listing cannabis as a soft narcotic, and two countries, the Netherlands and Uruguay, provide for special cannabis-related rules. While in the Netherlands marijuana is still classified as an illicit substance, these two countries tolerate and regulate the use of cannabis. Other jurisdictions provide for less strict or suspended punishment, or substitute traditional punishment with voluntary addiction treatment, community work, or other forms of alternative punishment if someone is caught using or dealing soft drugs. Additionally, New Zealand regulates the production and sale of so-called "new psychoactive substances," such as party pills and synthetic cannabis. Previously unregulated and sold without restrictions, these drugs recently became subject to government control, including the regulation of their sale. In Germany, even though drugs are divided into different schedules, for law enforcement purposes all narcotics are treated equally, and the distinction between soft and hard drugs can only be considered at sentencing, taking into account associated risks and damages.

In all of the countries reviewed such drug-related offenses as distributing drugs, possessing them in large amounts, cultivating plants containing a narcotic substance, producing drugs and possessing items for their production, etc., are recognized as crimes. Meanwhile, the possession of drugs for personal use in small amounts is no longer a criminal offense in some jurisdictions, but rather a misdemeanor subject to a monetary fine or other nonpecuniary punishment. These jurisdictions include Brazil, the Czech Republic, Norway, Portugal, and the Australian Capital Territory. An interesting example is provided by Costa Rica where the use of narcotics, including personal use, is prohibited by law but no penalty for this violation is found in the Criminal Code. In Argentina, the possession of narcotics remains illegal but the Supreme Court has ruled that "private actions of individuals are exempt from the authority of judges as long as they do not offend or injure others," declaring penalties against an adult who consumed marijuana unconstitutional.

Costa Rica, Germany, Israel, New Zealand, and the Australian State of New South Wales are among those jurisdictions where the police, prosecutors, or courts have discretion to drop charges if a minor offense involving prohibited drugs has been committed for the first time and the accused person is willing to undergo addiction treatment.

The possession and use of narcotics is a crime under the laws of most of the countries included in this report. However, in some countries medical treatment is prescribed for those found in violation of drug laws or can be chosen by the accused person as an alternative to traditional punishment. Mexican law requires that individuals found in possession of limited quantities of narcotics be referred to addiction treatment programs. In Norway a minor drug offender can opt to enroll in a drug treatment program instead of going to prison, but violation of the treatment program conditions will place the offender in jail. In Argentina a judge may replace imprisonment by detoxification and rehabilitation treatment. Special treatment for children is prescribed by the laws of New Zealand.

It appears that where decriminalization of drug-related activities has occurred, it was done with the purpose of securing the health and safety of the individual and the public. Even in those countries where the use of some drugs is allowed (Uruguay), advertising or promoting drugs, or consuming them in a public place, is prohibited. Dutch legislation emphasizes that coffee shops are prohibited from advertising drugs and causing a nuisance. The reduction of harm from drug use is the declared purpose for the creation of varied medical and social service facilities (e.g., needle exchanges, drug consumption rooms). However, even the authorization of such services by law (Germany, Netherlands, Portugal) has not resulted in the legalization of narcotics.

Information on pending proposals for the legalization of cannabis in Canada and South Africa, and decriminalization of the possession of small amounts of heroin, cocaine, and cannabis for personal use in Ireland, is also included in the report.

Periodical and Internet Sources Bibliography

The following articles have been selected to supplement the diverse views presented in this chapter.

Katherine Beckett, "The Uses and Abuses of Police Discretion: Toward Harm Reduction Policing," Harvard Law & Policy Review, 2016, http://harvardlpr.com/wp-content/uploads/2016/02/10.1_6_Beckett.pdf

Anthony Braga, "The New Policing, Crime Control, and Harm Reduction," NYU Furman Center, July 2017, http://furmancenter.org/research/iri/essay/the-new-policing-crime-control-and-harm-reduction.

David Cloud and Chelsea Davis, "What Congress Lifting the Ban on Needle Exchange Programming Could Mean for Law Enforcement," Vera Institute for Justice, January 12, 2016, https://www.vera.org/blog/what-congress-lifting-the-federal-ban-on-needle-exchange-programming-could-mean-for-law-enforcement.

Diane Goldstein, "Harm Reduction Can Help to Heal Law Enforcement's Rift with the Public," Pacific Standard, June 23, 2015, https://psmag.com/news/harm-reduction-can-help-to-heal-law-enforcements-rift-with-the-public.

Harm Reduction Coalition, "Police Issues and Concerns," Harm Reduction Coalition, n.d., http://harmreduction.org/wp-content/uploads/2012/01/Police-HR-Concerns.pdf.

North Carolina Harm Reduction Coalition, "An Interview with Corporal D.A. Jackson from the Guilford County Sheriff," NCHRC, 2018, http://www.nchrc.org/law-enforcement/law-enforcement-voices/articles/.

Jessica Reichert and Lily Gleicher, "Rethinking Law Enforcement's Role on Drugs: Community Drug Intervention and Diversion Efforts," Illinois Criminal Justice Information Authority, January 25, 2017, http://www.icjia.state.il.us/articles/rethinking-law-enforcement-s-role-on-drugs-community-drug-intervention-and-diversion-efforts.

For Further Discussion

Chapter 1

1. The US Department of Health and Human Services maintains that users need a combination of medicine and behavioral intervention to stop their addictions. After reading all the viewpoints in this chapter, what else might patients in harm reduction therapy need and why?
2. "Meet the patient where he or she is" is a harm reduction philosophy. In what ways do some of the contributors argue that medical professionals get in the way of putting this philosophy in effective action?
3. Do you think that diversity training during medical school can help future medical professionals identify and understand their own unconscious biases? Why or why not?

Chapter 2

1. Why should universal healthcare be a guaranteed right for all Americans?
2. Should syringe exchange programs be allowed throughout the United States? What benefits could they have? What downsides could they introduce?
3. How does DrugRehab.org use statistics to argue its premise that drug addiction affects everyone? Is the use of statistics effective in argumentation?

Chapter 3

1. AlcoholAnswers.org maintains harm reduction needs different measurement outcomes than other treatment strategies. What are they? How and why are they different?
2. Dr. Jana Burson presents an imagined dialogue between Harm Reduction and Abstinence-Only. As you read their

arguments, do you find one more convincing than another? Which ones are they and why do they work?

3. Scott Kellogg proposes a gradualism approach to recovery from addiction. He cites the findings of other researchers. How do they help or hinder his argument?

Chapter 4

1. What are the benefits of encouraging greater cooperation between law enforcement and public health agencies? Any drawbacks?

2. How does the US Office of Drug Control Policy affect harm reduction?

3. The Library of Congress compared drug laws across sixteen countries. What commonalities and differences did it find? How do you think America stacks up?

Organizations to Contact

The editors have compiled the following list of organizations concerned with the issues debated in this book. The descriptions are derived from materials provided by the organizations. All have publications or information available for interested readers. The list was compiled on the date of publication of the present volume; the information provided here may change. Be aware that many organizations take several weeks or longer to respond to inquiries, so allow as much time as possible.

American Psychological Association

750 First Street, NE
Washington, DC 20002-4242
800-374-2721
website: www.apa.org

The American Psychological Association represents psychology in America with more than 100,000 researchers, educators, clinicians, consultants, and students among its membership. It is the leading scientific and professional psychological organization in the United States. It publishes many articles in its journals, magazines, and website regarding harm reduction.

Harm Reduction Coalition

22 West 27th Street, 5th Floor
New York, NY 10001
212-213-6376
email: hrc@harmreduction.org
1111 Broadway, 3rd floor
Oakland, CA 94607
510-285-2799
email: hrcwest@harmreduction.org
website: www.harmreduction.org

The Harm Reduction Coalition was founded in 1993 by a working group of needle exchange providers, advocates, and drug users. The organization has grown into a broad network of people working together to combat the stereotypes of drug users. It also campaigns for reform in policy and public health.

Institute for Behavior and Health

6191 Executive Boulevard
Rockville, MD 20852
301-231-9010
email: ContactUs@IBHinc.org
website: www.ibhinc.org

The Institute for Behavior and Health is a nonprofit organization that strives to reduce illegal drug use and improve health in America's communities. Founded in 1978, it conducts research to develop new ideas advocated at meetings and in published reports. In this way, it works as a change agent in public health.

Law Enforcement and HIV Network

email: leahn@leahn.org
website: www.leahn.org

The Law Enforcement and HIV Network (LEAHN) connects public health professionals and law enforcement to prevent HIV and substance abuse. It helps to build partnerships both locally and globally to aid people who inject drugs. Many of its programs are based on harm reduction strategies.

National Center for Biotechnology Information

8600 Rockville Pike
Bethesda, MD 20894
website: www.ncbi.nlm.nih.gov

The National Center for Biotechnology Information (NCBI) is a governmental organization founded in 1988 as part of the National Library of Medicine within the National Institutes of Health. Its mission is to uncover and disseminate new information on medicine, health, and disease. Through its databases, it offers many harm reduction resources.

North Carolina Harm Reduction Coalition

3953-A Market Street
Building B
Wilmington, NC 28403
336-543-8050
email: robert.bb.childs@gmail.com
website: www.nchrc.org

The North Carolina Harm Reduction Coalition offers support programs and services to people impacted by drug use, overdose, and HIV, as well as other conditions. It also provides support to provider, public health, and law enforcement. It works toward syringe exchange, syringe decriminalization, and public policy reform.

Open Society Foundations

224 West 57th Street
New York, NY 10019
212-548-0600
website: www.opensocietyfoundations.org

Open Society Foundations was founded by philanthropist George Soros in 1979. He has donated more than $32 billion to fund programs in more than one hundred countries. Its mission is to hold governments accountable for their actions. As part of its mission, it advocates for harm reduction.

Substance Abuse and Mental Health Services Association

5600 Fishers Lane
Rockville, MD 20857
877-SAMHSA-7
website: samhsa.gov

The Substance Abuse and Mental Health Services Administration (SAMHSA) is an agency within the US Department of Health and Human Services (HHS) focused on public and behavioral health of America. A key component of its mission is to lessen the effect of substance abuse on American communities.

Office of the Surgeon General

U.S. Department of Health and Human Services
200 Independence Avenue SW
Humphrey Bldg. Suite 701H
Washington, DC 20201
202-205-0143
email: ashmedia@hhs.gov
website: www.surgeongeneral.gov

The Office of the Surgeon General is home to the Surgeon General, America's official doctor. In 2016, Surgeon General, Dr. Vivek Murthy, issued a comprehensive report dealing with the country's drug epidemic, "Facing Addiction in America: The Surgeon General's Report on Alcohol, Drugs, and Health." This report is the first ever issued by a Surgeon General on substance use and addiction and represented Dr. Murthy's priorities. He served from 2014–2017.

United Nations Office on Drugs and Crime

United Nations Headquarters
DC1 Building, Room 613
One United Nations Plaza
New York, NY 10017
212-963-5698
email: pasquali@un.org
website: www.unodc.org

The United Nations Office on Drugs and Crime formed in 1997 through the merger of individual organizations focused on drug control and crime. It seeks to educate governments to see drug use as a problem and not a crime. It also advocates against youth using illegal drugs and for people using drugs to get help.

Bibliography of Books

Mark O. Bigler. *Harm Reduction*. New York, NY: Oxford University Press, 2014.

Yuet W. Cheung, Patricia G. Erickson, Pat A. O'Hare, and Diane M. Riley (eds.). *Harm Reduction: A New Direction for Drug Policies and Programs*. Toronto, Canada; University of Toronto Press, 2016.

Patt Denning and Jeannie Little. *Over the Influence, Second Edition: The Harm Reduction Guide to Controlling Your Drug and Alcohol Use*. New York, NY: Guilford Press, 2017.

Maurice S. Fisher. *Harm Reduction for High-Risk Adolescent Substance Abusers*. Washington, DC: NASW Press, 2014.

Seán Foy. *Solution Focused Harm Reduction: Working Effectively with People Who Misuse Substances*. Cham, Switzerland: Palgrave Macmillan/Springer International Publishing, 2018.

Lucy Gell, Gerhard Buhringer, Jane McLeod, Sarah Forberger, John Holmes, Anne Lingford-Hughes, and Petra S. Meir (eds.). *What Determines Harm from Addictive Substances and Behaviors?* New York, NY: Oxford University Press, 2016.

Emi Koyama. *Reclaiming Harm Reduction*. Portland, OR: Confluere Publications, 2016.

Sylvia I. Mignon. Substance Abuse Treatment: Options, Challenges, and Effectiveness. New York, NY: Springer Publishing Company, 2015.

Meredith B. Morris. *Public Health and Harm Reduction: Principles, Perceptions and Programs*. New York, NY: Nova Science Publishers, 2015.

Stephen Parkin. *An Applied Visual Sociology: Picturing Harm Reduction.* London, UK: Routledge, 2016.

Imain Sahed and Antony Chaufton (eds.). Psychtropic Drugs, Prevention and Harm Reduction. London, UK: ISTE Press, 2017.

Christopher Smith and Zack Marshall (eds.). *Critical Approaches to Harm Reduction: Conflict, Institutionalization, (De)Politicization, and Direct Action.* New York, NY: Nova Science Publishers, 2016.

US Congress House of Representatives, Committee on Government Reform. *Harm Reduction or Harm Maintenance: Is There Such a Thing as Safe Drug Abuse?* Washington, DC: Government Printing Office, 2005.

Alex S. Vitale. *The End of Policing.* Brooklyn, NY: Verso, 2017.

Daniel Wolfe and Joanne Csete. *Harm Reduction.* New York, NY: Open Society Foundations, 2015.

Index

A

abstinence only, 12, 18, 25–26, 29, 30, 57–58, 72–73, 75, 77–78, 83–107, 109, 112, 117, 152, 156

addiction, 14, 19–20, 22–23, 25–30, 35–38, 41, 45, 58–64, 72–81, 83, 85–91, 93, 98, 108, 119, 135, 154, 155, 157, 161–162

Affordable Care Act (ACA), 15, 50–55

AIDS, 40, 112, 119, 129, 132–140, 150

alcohol, 14, 19–23, 28, 32, 37, 40–42, 57, 60–64, 72–76, 80, 82, 85, 89–96, 98–101, 106–109, 137, 147, 157

Alcoholics Anonymous (AA), 20, 72, 74–75, 85–86, 89, 92, 94–95, 107

B

Baker, Charlie, 40

buprenorphine, 15, 18, 22, 26, 28, 30, 73, 77, 79–83, 108, 119, 138

Burson, Jana, 77–84

C

Canada, 48, 160, 163

cancer, 24, 143

Castillo, Tessie, 31–34

Centers for Disease Control (CDC), 66, 68, 119

Civil War, 27

Cloud, David, 113–123

cocaine, 21–22, 76, 90, 109, 114, 116, 63

conservatism, 31–34

coping methods, 60, 75, 92, 101

Country Focal Points (CFPs), 129–130

crime, 27, 29, 59–60, 62–64, 76, 80, 88, 102, 115–116, 121, 127, 130, 138–139, 154, 147, 161–162

criminal justice system, 19, 21, 23, 27, 32–34, 37, 41, 60, 63–64, 112–141, 148, 152, 155–157, 162

Crofts, Nick, 124–141

cycle of addiction, 26

D

decriminalization, 159–163

depressants, 28

detox, 18, 35, 37–41, 59, 83, 162

DiClementi, Jeannie D., 65–70

disability, 36, 115, 117, 147

Drug Abuse Resistance Education (DARE), 155

Drug-Free Communities (DFC), 154

drug-free society, 62, 72–74

Drug Policy Alliance, 62, 152–158

drug seeking, 38

DSM-IV, 100

E

e-cigarettes, 14, 18, 105

emergency rooms, 15, 18, 118

F

federal government budget, 152–157

fentanyl, 28, 38

Fiedler, Matthew, 51, 52, 54

Food and Drug Administration (FDA), 22, 28, 30, 80

France, 47, 49

G

Germany, 47–48, 160–163

Glauser, Wendy, 35–38

Gostin, Lawrence O., 142–151

Government Accountability Office (GAO), 156

gradualism, 72, 98–99, 102–104, 109

Great Britain, 47

H

Hammid, Julia, 85–88

Harm Reduction, Abstinence, and Moderation Support (HAMS), 94

Harm Reduction and Safety Recovery Plan, 15, 55–58

Harm Reduction Coalition, 29, 31–32, 104–105, 114

Harm Reduction principles, 29, 73, 84, 104, 117

Harrison Narcotics Act, 27

health care, 11, 15–16, 19–21, 23, 37–38, 41, 47, 49–54, 60–64, 114,, 116, 119, 143–145, 148–149

Health Care Marketplace, 20

health care system, 15, 23, 62–63, 148

health insurance, 47, 49–53, 149

hepatitis B, 66, 69, 99, 119

hepatitis C (HCV), 14, 29, 37, 66, 69, 79, 102, 119

heroin, 21–22, 27–28, 36, 38, 61, 90–91, 100, 114, 116, 120, 138, 163

High Intensity Drug Trafficking Areas (HIDTA), 154

HIV, 16, 24, 29, 37, 40, 65–69, 78–79, 99–100, 102, 112, 117, 119, 120, 124–129, 131, 133–140, 150, 156

homelessness, 36, 61, 64, 115, 117

I

Indiana, 65–66, 68–69, 79

injection drug use (IDU), 42, 65–67, 78, 117, 119

inpatient treatment facilities, 74, 83–84

Institute of Family Health, 15, 55–56

Institute of Medicine (IOM), 79, 143

J

Jardine, Melissa, 124–131

Johnson, Lyndon B., 45, 49

Joint Commission on Accreditation of Healthcare Organizations, 27

R

racial bias, 15, 18, 41

Rational Recovery, 74, 93, 107

Reagan, Ronald, 33

Recovery Support Services (RSS), 22

Reichel, Chloe, 39–42

remission, 19, 23

S

Sanders, Bernie, 46–49

Santhanam, Laura, 50–54

screening, 21, 23, 69, 150

self-medication, 60, 101

Shimkus, John, 52

SMART Recovery, 93, 107

social services, 114, 117, 119

Suboxone, 18

syringe exchange programs (SEPs), 18, 31, 43, 65–69, 78, 106, 114, 117, 119–120, 128, 163

T

Teitelbaum, Scott, 25–30

therapy, 14, 18, 21, 26, 37, 74, 77, 108, 138

Tierney, Mike, 35–38

treatment options, 19–24

Trump, Donald, 15, 50–55

tuberculosis (TB), 69

12-step programs, 28, 58, 75, 81–82, 87, 107

U

UF Health Florida Recovery Center, 25, 26

United Nations (UN), 112, 130, 139

U.S. Department of Health & Human Services, 29–24

V

Vermont, 46, 48

Vimont, Celia, 55–58

W

Walsh, Marty, 40

War on Drugs, 32, 33, 62, 114, 116

Wiley, Lindsay F., 142–151

withdrawal, 18, 22, 28, 36, 38, 80–81, 83

World Health Organization (WHO), 79, 117, 142

X

Xanax, 28